ENGLISH AS AN ADDITIONAL LANGUAGE

MEETING THE CHALLENGE IN THE CLASSROOM

Elizabeth Haslam, Edith Kellett and Yvonne Wilkin

David Fulton Publishers

David Fulton Publishers Ltd
The Chiswick Centre, 414 Chiswick High Road, London W4 5TF

www.fultonpublishers.co.uk

First published in Great Britain in 2005 by David Fulton Publishers

10 9 8 7 6 5 4 3 2 1

Note: The right of the authors to be identified as the authors of their work has been asserted by them in accordance with the Copyright, Designs and Patents Act 1988.

Copyright © Elizabeth Haslam, Edith Kellett and Yvonne Wilkin 2005

British Library Cataloguing in Publication Data
A catalogue record for this book is available from the British Library.

David Fulton Publishers is a division of Granada Learning, part of ITV plc.

ISBN 1 84312 186 7

Typeset by RefineCatch Ltd, Bungay, Suffolk
Printed and bound in Great Britain

Contents

Acknowledgements   iv

Introduction   v

Chapter 1   Stories about Precious and Jim   1

Chapter 2   How pupils make progress   9

Chapter 3   Exploring language and assessment   19

Chapter 4   Targets and teaching strategies   24

Chapter 5   Preparing for an EAL beginner   45

Chapter 6   Teaching a beginner   60

Chapter 7   Ways of moving on   71

Chapter 8   Developing CALP (Cognitive Academic Language Proficiency)   83

Accompanying CD   95

Glossary   97

Bibliography   99

Appendix: Finding out more   101

Index   106

Acknowledgements

We have set out to provide an easy guide to what is generally accepted as good practice: tried, tested and trusted approaches to use in schools with bilingual pupils. You will find some working suggestions you can use tomorrow, and some ideas which will help to shape your thoughts for a very long time.

Our thanks go to all the movers and shakers of language development work generally, who are the real brains behind this book. Thanks also go to the countless teachers and pupils whose experiences have informed or inspired what we have written for you.

A special thanks goes to NASSEA – the Northern Association of Support Services for Equality and Achievement – for allowing us to reproduce their extended Step Descriptors.

Last, but not least, thanks go to all those who gave us a hand with this, especially those who read parts of the text as the book developed.

Introduction

Who is this book for?

This book assumes no previous knowledge on the part of the reader in respect of teaching pupils who are learning through English as an additional language. It is a handbook which will, hopefully, help school staff to accommodate the needs of their pupils and meet the standards demanded by Ofsted. Even more hopefully, it will kindle curiosity about English as an Additional Language, a collection of knowledge, perspectives and skills which can inform and transform every aspect of practice.

This book is written with the individual practitioner in mind. Therefore, although it would be inadequate to write an EAL book with no references to the importance of whole-school initiatives and the ethos of the institution, the bulk of this text assumes that the individual will be concerned with what happens in the classroom, as that is the sphere of an individual teacher's influence and the centre of teaching activity. The school ethos has huge importance for pupils' health and progress, but it is not under the control of one individual. We will largely be concerned here with strategies and techniques that will be under the control of the individual teacher.

What is English as an Additional Language (EAL)?

This question generates a different answer from each practitioner! For the purposes of this publication, we will here define our concepts of EAL. First, the field of EAL is about learning and facilitating learning for pupils whose first language is not English. It embodies a culture, an approach, a mindset. There is a whole treasure trove of things one can know or discover about EAL, but it is the holistic, inclusive attitude to identifying and then meeting pastoral and academic needs which is the bedrock of good provision for these pupils.

A key part of this attitude is the understanding that we are all learners as well as teachers. We are good at identifying and capitalising on our pupils' prior knowledge, but sometimes we overlook our own information gaps, particularly in areas which are outside our previous experiences.

A useful image at this point would be Vygotsky's Zone of Proximal Development (ZPD), as the underlying principle has huge implications for classroom practice and has influenced many writers and thinkers in educational fields.

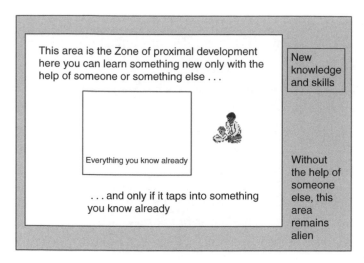

Figure 0.1 'Zone of Proximal Development'

Looking at this from an EAL perspective, a pupil arrives with his or her own culturally and linguistically relevant body of knowledge and experiences. Teachers approach the learning environment with their own knowledge, expertise and experiences. Where these are mutually respected and jointly acknowledged, a climate is created in which the pupil can thrive. Where the pupil's prior knowledge is not acknowledged, or is not evident to the teacher, curriculum interventions are likely to be inappropriate, resulting in significant pupil underachievement.

Is it just an attitude?

For the most comprehensive description of EAL yet published, you cannot beat NALDIC Working Paper 5 (NALDIC 1999). However, our task here is to provide a brief introduction which will be useful to the interested but busy. We will approach it, like all ZPD-aware teachers do, from what the learner already knows. What do *you* already know?

You are already well on the way to being an effective teacher of pupils with EAL if:

- you see beyond key vocabulary and are keenly aware of the language skills practised, language demands made and language learning opportunities presented in school;

- you know about teaching genres, about the relationship between oracy and literacy, and are familiar with strategies such as Directed Activities Related to Text;

- you know about relating visuals and practicals to the learning process;

- you are an expert in varying questioning techniques and are aware of the features associated with problem-solving tasks;

- you are skilled at including all pupils through a variety of differentiation strategies;

- you know about Thinking Skills, and about varying approaches to teaching and learning;

- you know about Competence/Performance distinction;

- you have an interest in cross-cultural communication, anti-racism and multi-culturalism;

- you are aware of the limitations of, and bias inherent in, standardised testing, and have a leaning towards a fuller, more dynamic assessment process;

- you understand the importance of the pastoral side of teaching and pay close attention to the ethos of the school and how it affects the learning and self-image of each pupil.

To be effective, provision for pupils with EAL must be a multifaceted, inclusive, cross-curricular approach affecting and informing every aspect of school life.

It follows that, whatever aspect of school life an educator is most concerned with, s/he will already be aware of some features of EAL work. Similarly, it follows that, however much we think we know, there is always more to discover in such a wide, fascinating area.

This breadth of focus can appear overwhelming. Perhaps this is why some sources tie EAL teaching tightly to the teaching of National Curriculum English. While teaching National Curriculum English is certainly an important activity, it is not the whole sum of EAL teaching work, much of which happens in other subjects, or is supported by the school ethos itself.

We hope that this book, and the accompanying CD, provides readers with guidance and inspiration – and also saves them some time!

The accompanying CD contains a variety of amendable resources for readers to download and print out. For a full list of contents see p. 95

CHAPTER 1

Stories about Precious and Jim

The story of Precious

Precious was a small black African child. She had been taken away from her country and most of her family. When she started school, in the Spring term, she spoke no English. She lived in a largely white area rife with racism and was taught by teachers who had never met an African before. She could be described as a very visible little person.

Precious was a bright, assertive individual who knew what she wanted and what she did not want. She had the same age-appropriate skills and knowledge as the children she had grown up with, but had never heard of Biff or Chip, Play-Doh or the Incy-Wincy spider. She had not been accustomed to cutting out or sticking in with a Pritt Stick. She blew her nose in a different way.

Precious did not always understand which activities were work and which were play. This meant she did not always realise which were voluntary and which were compulsory. Because she knew her own mind and had a will of iron, she voted with her feet whenever she perceived anything as tedious. Having already experienced more changes in her six years than any of the adults working with her could possibly imagine, she was unlikely to be easily impressed or persuaded to toe the line. Before long, she was regarded as 'difficult'.

Sensibly, her teacher realised Precious needed practical experiences. To accommodate this, it was decided that she should spend part of the day in another class, which was mixed age, in order to allow her access to the facilities in Reception. After a couple of months, a place became free in the mixed class and Precious was moved to it permanently. On her first morning, she went for her snack with the other pupils in the class. Like them, she looked for a laminated card with her name on it. Unlike them, she did not find one. Nobody had had time to make her one. Precious walked around the tables until told to sit down somewhere. It must have seemed to her that she had been kicked out of her previous class and then not welcomed in her new one. Had she been older and bigger, no doubt the teachers would have soon known just how she felt.

The insensitivity shown to this child could be seen as a type of institutional racism and/or a lack of the empathy possessed by all good teachers.

What can be done for our children like Precious? The main character in our next story should be able to help.

The story of Jim

Who is Jim?

> Jim Cummins teaches in the Department of Curriculum, Teaching and Learning of the University of Toronto. His research focuses on the challenges educators face in adjusting to classrooms where cultural and linguistic diversity is the norm.

This information comes from the cover of Jim Cummins' *Negotiating Identities: Education for empowerment in a diverse society* (revised 2001 edition), a highly influential book which we strongly recommend to interested teachers. He is one of the best-known writers in the field of English as an Additional Language and his influence lies both in what we earlier described as the 'holistic, inclusive attitude' and in more obviously practical applications, such as his cognitive framework, which we discuss below.

First, if we may make a gross simplification of his insights, Cummins champions the rights of the pupils to their own languages and cultures. He points out that we need to respond to the way that the pupils view the world and to give them platforms on which to interact with the world on their own terms and in their own ways. He advises us that empowering our pupils is the true business of the teacher. He has a great deal to say about the power relations at work in education:

> Coercive relations of power are reflected in and shaped through the use of language or discourse and usually involve a definitional process that legitimates the inferior or deviant status accorded to the subordinated group . . . The process of defining groups or individuals as inferior or deviant almost inevitably results in a pattern of interactions that restricts their development and potential.
>
> (Cummins 1996: 14)

What Cummins is saying here is that there are plenty of ways of being and doing. If our classrooms only recognise one way, possibly a white middle-class way, then anyone not belonging to that group will be described as wrong or bad in some way because they will not fit the norms that apply to that group. Being described as wrong or bad will result in pupils being restricted in some way, which was what happened to Precious.

Had Precious been in Jim Cummins' class, he would have:

- found out about the skills and knowledge she had already developed and capitalised on them;
- made culturally familiar resources available to her;
- engineered her acceptance into the group with sensitivity, giving her time to acquire new skills and new general knowledge;
- developed positive images of Africa and Africans with the class;
- understood that education is, first and foremost, a social activity, happening in a society and being about a society;
- presented her with learning tasks in a mode which meant something to her;
- allowed her to respond in her way, not his.

One of the reasons Jim's work has been so popular is his practical approach. His 'framework to identify cognitive involvement in language tasks and activities' has been used in many ways by various authorities. For the original, we refer

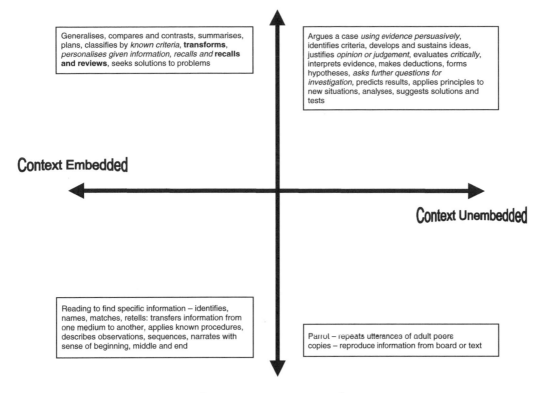

High Cognitive Demand

Generalises, compares and contrasts, summarises, plans, classifies by *known criteria*, **transforms**, *personalises given information, recalls and* **recalls and reviews**, seeks solutions to problems

Argues a case *using evidence persuasively*, identifies criteria, develops and sustains ideas, justifies *opinion or judgement*, evaluates *critically*, interprets evidence, makes deductions, forms hypotheses, *asks further questions for investigation*, predicts results, applies principles to new situations, analyses, suggests solutions and tests

Context Embedded

Context Unembedded

Reading to find specific information – identifies, names, matches, retells: transfers information from one medium to another, applies known procedures, describes observations, sequences, narrates with sense of beginning, middle and end

Parrot – repeats utterances of adult peers
copies – reproduce information from board or text

Low Cognitive Demand

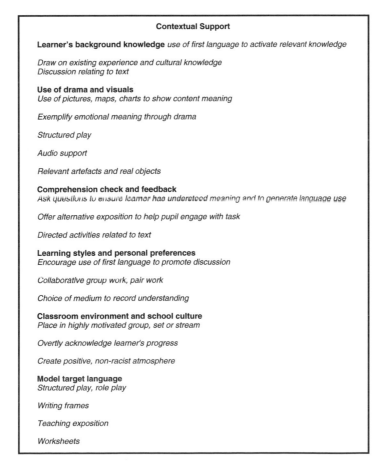

Contextual Support

Learner's background knowledge *use of first language to activate relevant knowledge*

Draw on existing experience and cultural knowledge
Discussion relating to text

Use of drama and visuals
Use of pictures, maps, charts to show content meaning

Exemplify emotional meaning through drama

Structured play

Audio support

Relevant artefacts and real objects

Comprehension check and feedback
Ask questions to ensure learner has understood meaning and to generate language use

Offer alternative exposition to help pupil engage with task

Directed activities related to text

Learning styles and personal preferences
Encourage use of first language to promote discussion

Collaborative group work, pair work

Choice of medium to record understanding

Classroom environment and school culture
Place in highly motivated group, set or stream

Overtly acknowledge learner's progress

Create positive, non-racist atmosphere

Model target language
Structured play, role play

Writing frames

Teaching exposition

Worksheets

Figure 1.1   The Cummins Framework as used by Tameside

- Reads for specific information
- Identifies, names, matches, retells
- Transfers information from one medium to another
- Applies known procedures
- Describes observations
- Sequences
- Narrates with a sense of beginning, middle and end

Figure 1.2   The jigsaw puzzler

you to *Negotiating Identities*. The diagram on the previous page is the version used in many Tameside schools.

The Framework is based on two intersecting continua, one of which maps the degree of difficulty, while the other indicates the amount of support provided. The resulting four areas are specific zones which can be used for differentiation. Precious, in those early months, needed to operate in the bottom left zone, which means her work would have been simple, with good support. In Tameside, this is called the 'Jigsaw Puzzler' because the pupils are involved in putting things together, rather than changing them or inventing them.

Teachers planning for Precious using the Cummins Framework would be likely to choose activities like these:

- Finding her name in a list of other names.

- Matching games using her friends' names, possibly with photos as a support.

- Listening to stories in her own language on a tape.

- Joining in with action songs in English, especially ones using some real meanings like 'Heads, shoulders, knees and toes'.

- Naming items in the pictures of a book chosen to be culturally appropriate for all the class, e.g. a story about school or the local area.

- Making her own book about her own school, with labels.

- Activities to practise cutting, drawing and sticking.

Because Precious is operating in another language, she already has an intellectual task – translating and learning new vocabulary and grammatical structures. At this stage, she does not need an additional burden, so her work carries a low intellectual demand. She is mostly being asked to copy, match, remember and name. The support she needs does not have to be a person; putting the work into a known context will often be enough. She will, therefore, look at pictures of familiar things and people, which should relate to real life *as she knows it*. Too many resources for young children reflect an imaginary world of fantasy farm-yards and shell-strewn beaches. These are a kind of code some children learn from the cradle, but Precious will not know it, and neither will some of the other, English-speaking children in the class. If this sounds odd, ask yourself when you last saw a real dog in a real kennel, when you last saw a pig in a sty, and how many times you remember playing in the snow at Christmas. These images are con-structs, and learning them can get in the way of learning other things. Precious will be using, therefore, photos of her own school, the nearest shops, the road outside and the people she meets in school. From this she will move on to pictures of, for example, schools, roads, vehicles, shops and parks in books. Later, she might be ready for images of snowmen at Christmas and cheerful ducks in ponds, but at the moment she needs things which are always true and make obvious sense.

She will also be offered resources in her own language and images relating to her earlier life. Other support will come from her peers. Engaging in collaborative practical work will be the fastest way for her to improve the craft skills she will need for the rest of Key Stage 1. She will also develop social English much faster when engaged in a group or paired task.

Basing our planning on the advice of Jim Cummins offers Precious a much better deal. There are other important stories to listen to as well, however.

The Partnership story

The Partnership Pack (NFER/DES 1990) suggests structures and strategies useful for working together. Its 'partnership cycle' has been particularly helpful in shaping working arrangements for those planning and teaching together. It is reprinted here by permission from HMSO.

Partnership teaching is an excellent way of sharing and increasing expertise, thus enabling mutual support and ensuring appropriate use of everyone's time. It facilitates the fullest use of support staff, who can be underused or deskilled in

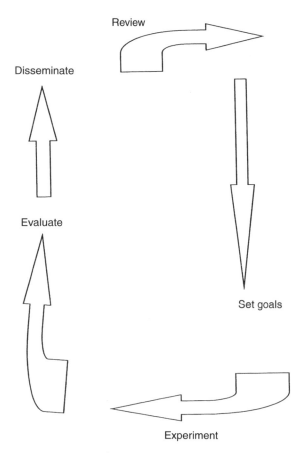

Figure 1.3 The partnership cycle (Reproduced by permission of Her Majesty's Stationery Office)

situations without clear parameters. When operating well, the partnership cycle results in a common base of resources, strategies and skills. At best, it is personally and professionally stimulating for those involved. It is at its best in settings where there is good management support, allowing meeting and planning time for those involved. Where such support is not present, the system can, however, still operate with some degree of success, as, with a little imagination, it lends itself to appropriate interpretations.

What could partnership work have done for Precious? If her teacher had had another adult to work with, especially one with an interest in EAL teaching, following a partnership cycle would have helped them to organise their work and would have provided a professional framework to enable them to share ideas and techniques. The open exchange of opinion encouraged within the partnership cycle could have enabled another adult to give Precious's class teacher a more appropriate perspective, and there would have been opportunities to develop a classroom inclusive of her needs.

One of the strategies suggested as part of such a partnership would certainly have been collaborative group work, as this is closely associated with all kinds of partnership arrangements. Collaborative group work is effective for language development and for enabling access to the curriculum. It differs from the usual models of group work or pair work in that it always involves some kind of information exchange and that information is transferred from one medium of communication to another. This ensures the repetition, support and reinforcement which are so beneficial for all pupils. It is, incidentally, highly enjoyable too. The Collaborative Learning Project is one good source of ideas and information about this kind of activity (see Useful Contacts, p. 102).

The story of the Race Relations (Amendment) Act

It is a sobering thought that failing to understand or meet Precious's needs is now officially no longer an unfortunate error, but an instance of institutional racism. Pupils in situations similar to Precious's are vulnerable and isolated. In schools with small numbers of ethnic minority pupils, there may be more barriers to learning; therefore the individual teacher carries an even greater responsibility. The content of the Act requires all schools to publish a race equality policy, and then to monitor its effectiveness. Therefore, even in schools with very few or no ethnic minority pupils, teachers have a responsibility to understand minority and EAL issues, and to put appropriate policies into practice.

> Institutional racism is the failure of an organisation to provide a service to people because of their colour, culture, faith or ethnic origin. It can be detected in processes, attitudes and behaviours which disadvantage minority ethnic people.
>
> (Race Relations (Amendment) Act, 2000)

For schools, this means that ignorance of these matters is not acceptable. As teachers, we need to be clear about the processes, attitudes and behaviours operating in our classrooms.

Assuming Precious is in a school which adheres to the law, her teacher should be able to find a helpful policy, with some guidelines for practice to back it up. There may be ways of using the policy to gain resources – of time, materials or staff support. Hopefully, the policy will have had a positive effect on the ethos of the school, enabling it to embrace the hidden diversity that is found even in seemingly monolingual all-white neighbourhoods.

In order to avoid the institutional racism which can warp school experiences for a child like Precious, we need to examine her needs:

- All children need security. Children who have been uprooted and who may have suffered trauma need certainty.

- All children benefit from a routine they can understand. Children who have to function in a foreign environment using a foreign language, need a solid, predictable routine.

- All children need to sense they belong. If we cannot show that they belong by what we say to them, we must be sure to show them by the things we do.

- All children need appropriate learning experiences. We get back from them only their reactions to our actions and what they can do with what we put in.

Security, routine, a sense of belonging and appropriate teaching methods. Precious's needs were not so different from those of the rest of her class, just more urgent than some. Precious's story illustrates the importance of understanding the pupil's experience and how this will affect the pupil's view of events in the classroom. When we cannot understand what people say to us, we are doubly conscious of how they look, how they act and their tone of voice. That which to an English speaker sounds businesslike or neutral in tone can sound angry or unfriendly to someone who is not familiar with the language. We all know that actions which we perceive as unimportant can assume major proportions to a child. This is hugely magnified when that child already feels disconnected from the group in some way.

The story of the strategies

As the education strategies have developed, more information has been given on teaching EAL. Mainstream acceptance of some ideas and techniques associated with EAL teaching is a positive development. It is, however, important to recognise that EAL issues are wider than can be promoted within individual strategies. Precious's teachers should, therefore, be able to find at least some of the information they need from official documents and regular visitors to the school. They will have to put the pieces together themselves, however. It may comfort them to see a wider application peeping through the development of the Primary Strategy. Real breadth of interpretation is vital to EAL teaching. Following narrower advice limits this activity to a small part of the school experience, leaving some very important issues unaddressed and some much-needed opportunities ignored.

The story of the EAL teachers

Now we have looked at so many stories associated with EAL provision, it is time to share our own story, which we believe would help Precious's teacher. It is made up from all the other stories and we think it complements them well. It is this:

The key elements of teaching EAL as we see them are as follows:

- Anti-racism.

- Language exists within context; we need to be aware of this when assessing and planning. Therefore
    - i skills are practised and language is taught in a meaningful context, rather than in isolation, drawing on and reinforcing the National Curriculum, and
    - ii we use context-embedded teaching to support meaning, and we build on responses to support further production.

- There is a distinction between social and academic English.

- The pupil's prior knowledge and experience should be accessed, used and built on.

- Oracy and collaboration.

The first of these is discussed briefly here: the others are examined in detail in the forthcoming chapters.

Anti-racism

There is a great deal of useful literature offering good advice on anti-racism, a topic too large for this book. What is appropriate to mention here, however, are those elements under the control of the individual teacher:

- Be aware of your school's policies. These are the frameworks that underpin the rest of your work.

- Make sure you create equal access opportunities for parents and pupils. These are opportunities which take their needs and situations into account.

- Promote anti-racism in your classroom as part of an ethos valuing individuality and fairness. Deal with incidents promptly. Be clear about the definition of a racist incident – the key lies in the victim's perceptions.

- Be aware of cultural and ethnicity issues. Do not make assumptions. Let parents know that you take an interest.

- Ensure that your information on ethnicity is accurate. Track pupils' attainment. Do not confuse EAL with SEN.

SUMMARY

The first key concept of teaching children with EAL is an ethos which gives rise to a vigorous anti-racist approach. The most basic manifestation of this is an attitude of care which takes into account the pupils' experiences, situations and cultures.

CHAPTER 2

How pupils make progress

In this chapter, we shall be looking at the kinds of progress we expect to see in a developing bilingual pupil. We start by looking at a real pupil. Comma arrived part-way through Year 6. His preferred language was Cantonese, but he had been learning English in Hong Kong, so he arrived able to read straightforward passages with understanding and he had beautiful English handwriting. He was not confident enough to construct anything but the most simple sentences without prompts or encouragement. He was naturally taciturn with both children and adults, so his speech was the least developed of his English skills, and he tended to be unresponsive. For the rest of the year, he made steady progress in increasing his vocabulary and understanding of what was expected of him in the school. In September, he moved to the High School. What follows is a classroom observation.

Geography (October, Y7)

Comma looked confident on entering the classroom. He seemed happy. He responded to a complex series of practical instructions promptly and correctly. He did not respond to open-ended prompts such as 'Tell me about it'. He responded (unwillingly) to simple closed questions about the model he had made. He gave minimal responses in social conversation. He followed the teacher's instructions and asked for no individual attention or help of any kind, although he did not complete all the work easily or correctly

The class had to look up items in an index. Comma did this quickly and seemed to find it easy. He could use the index to find the right page of the Atlas. He found it difficult, however, to locate specific features on the map. He did not volunteer any answers, although he knew at least one of them.

The class then did some work on the British Isles. Comma began straight away. He had understood the gist of what he had to do, but had missed some of the verbal and written instructions. He had understood about the country borders and he knew the names and locations of the countries.

Significant facts from this observation are:

● Comma was functioning without in-class support. His behaviour suggests that extra adult attention in the classroom would only have made him uncomfortable. Some parts of the lesson were very supportive of Comma, because there were strong visual and practical aspects to the lesson and much of the language and behaviour expected of Comma was modelled for him.

- Comma arrived looking confident and happy. He had made a model like all the other pupils and he completed an appropriate amount of work during the lesson. In many ways, he was fitting in.

- He understood social conversation because he gave correct responses. He was not ready to join in for long, or able to speak in longer utterances.

- He understood how to use the Atlas index quickly and efficiently.

- He understood straightforward questions like 'What is this?' 'Where is it?' 'What is it made of?' Although he preferred not to speak in class, he responded correctly in short phrases when the teacher asked him these simple questions personally.

- When the independent written work began, Comma's behaviour showed that he had been able to pick up the gist of what was required of him. He had therefore accessed the most basic level of the work. Comma would probably have attained a higher level if the work had been in Cantonese, or if he had communicated more freely with the teacher or other pupils.

What is significant in the above list is not just Comma's growing use of English, but a whole parcel of issues. They influence the relationship between Comma and the lesson in terms of language, content and social environment. They may be easier to see as a diagram (see opposite).

When observing pupils learning through EAL with a view to assessment or identifying support needs, it is not just vocabulary and syntax which are significant, but the whole picture – which we can describe as 'language behaviour'. This is an appropriate term because we are not just watching out for what Comma says and writes, but for how he responds, how he functions and how he moves on. Not all of these are expressed in language, but, because Comma is a developing bilingual pupil, we know they will always be closely connected to his acquisition of English.

In observation, in assessment and in planning and teaching, then, we need to take into account not just language, but language behaviour. Consider the language behaviour typical of a pupil new to English in the next example.

Art lesson, Reception (one week after arrival)

When the teacher gave the class instructions, Litotes watched the other pupils and copied them. She did not speak to any of the other children, but she did pretend to shoot some of them with a toy bow and arrow. When talking to me, she could name 'Scissors' and 'Paper'. She asked for them using a gesture. She was able to say 'Yes' and 'Mine'. Like the other pupils, she made a simple paper flower.

At playtime, she skipped out and joined in with other children who were balancing on a log. She did not appear at all shy. Some of the children approached her, making a fuss and trying to pet her. Each time she ran away. An older boy approached her. She pushed him away, then pushed him all around the playground, laughing. She tried to join in with some pupils who were skipping, but they were finishing the game. She did not seem to understand it was time to go in.

On the carpet, she played with her flowers, not looking or listening to the teacher. She joined in when two girls started rocking. She pulled faces at another

Coping with social demands, making friends, being polite

Coping with the practical demands – homework, equipment, finding the classroom, using the school

Coping on an emotional level – feeling confident, being motivated

Coping on a cultural level – understanding a curriculum largely an expression of British/European general knowledge and cultural references

Understanding instructions and explanations

Acquiring and retaining new skills

Transferring the skills and knowledge acquired through education in Hong Kong into an English setting

Comma

Responding by complying with instructions, by giving a verbal contribution, or by writing/drawing as requested

Communicating in spoken and written English

Figure 2.1 Comma

pupil. When asked to tidy the shells, she went and stood by them, not clear about what she had to do.

Apart from showing an unusual degree of assertiveness (and mischief), Litotes' behaviour is fairly typical of a new pupil just starting to learn English:

- She watches other pupils and may copy what they do.

- She responds to some speech (e.g. she knew she had to do something with the shells).

- She learns the names of things she needs most frequently, or the expressions she needs to use (e.g. 'Mine!').

- She communicates by gesture (and, in Litotes' case, other physical means).

- She can perform a task suitable to her age and previous experiences if the English language demands are not too great.

- She misunderstands routines and expressions so she can feel slighted or mistreated without good cause (e.g. when she thought she had been excluded from the skipping game).

- She watches for visual clues to help her understand what is going on, she needs smiles, gestures, examples, pictures.

The beginning of a new pupil's journey into English, then, is about the physical, the visual and the straightforward. New pupils may be dependent on peer support, support through differentiation, or adult support in some situations. They may be able to react appropriately to the demands of the classroom. They may communicate a little, or only with certain people, or maybe not at all. Therefore these are the aspects of their language behaviour which we need to consider in order to assess their progress.

As can be seen by comparing Litotes with Comma, a great deal will depend on the pupil's own disposition and previous experience. Some of it will also be age-related. A child new to English in the Foundation stage may be functioning at an age-appropriate level when standing next to another pupil, exploring the materials without speaking, and would not cause a stir by staying at that level for a while. A young person recently arrived in Year 10, however, would be expected to make a conscious effort to communicate after an initial settling-in period.

The model of progress teachers can expect from pupils learning through English as an additional language is a journey from silence, or near-silence, to communication and then on to accurate, sophisticated use of academic English. It goes from dependence, or near dependence on others to complete independence, and maybe on to leadership skills. Figure 2.2 is an illustration of how pupils' progress in learning English will be expressed in various types of language behaviour.

Figure 2.2 shows the progress from:

- concrete → abstract
- dependent → independent
- withdrawn → communicative
- receptive → productive

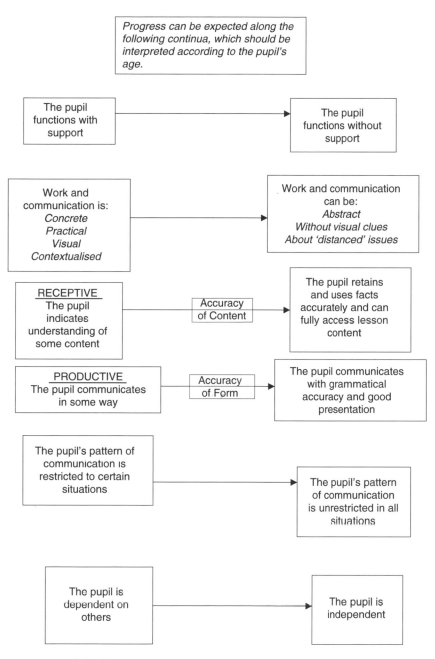

Figure 2.2 A model of learning progress

It should be noted that, in some situations, non-verbal communication can be regarded as a kind of production. Comma, for example, though unwilling to speak to his teacher beyond squeezing out a few grudging phrases, will proudly show her how hard he is working and how much he has understood by completing as much of his work as he can. Litotes expresses her desire to be one of the herd instead of a school pet by her physical responses to fussing and by her mischievous behaviour with her peers. In terms of language behaviour, Litotes and Comma are 'producing' because they are relating to those around them, making choices and acting on them, even on those occasions where they have not produced any English words.

It is also important to discuss at this point the distinctions between communication and communication with accuracy. As pupils begin to move into English, they will follow some of the same steps they followed when they acquired their first language. The need to communicate will be the driving force, so their first utterances will be like Litotes' – pointing and saying 'Scissors', by which we understand she would like us to pass her the scissors, please. Within a calendar year, a bright, outgoing pupil like her will be communicating all kinds of things with great effectiveness. She will be a fluent communicator in social English as well as in her first language. She may have all her facts accurate as well. She will not yet be an accurate communicator, however.

The movement from silence, or near silence, to the ability to communicate runs first to fluency, which implies an ease of communication unattainable in the early months, then to grammatical or syntactic accuracy and on to age-appropriate academic English. These last stages are harder to achieve and take longer to reach. They are also developmental. Age-appropriate academic language is very different at KS 4 than at KS 1. What this continuum does for us as teachers, however, is to enable us to see the movement from saying 'Scissors!' to 'Give scissor, please' as progress. It would be a mistake to view 'Give scissor, please' as inadequate in some way because it is not accurately expressed or regular English syntax. If we look at language progress in terms of movement through stages of increasing competence, fluency and accuracy, if we draw a distinction between factual and syntactic accuracy, then we can regard 'Give scissor, please' as a step forward.

From this, it can be seen that some progress bilingual pupils make will not show up on routine assessments in school. That is why observation in different contexts is important during assessment. To assess pupils' language behaviour, we need to see them in Art, at break, in Science, with a book, with other pupils and with adults, known and unknown. We need to know if they can make a suggestion in a group, if they can follow the gist of a teacher's explanation to a class, if they can find the relevant information in a textbook. Chapter 4 will describe an assessment system that uses the National Curriculum as a starting point, and therefore fits in well with existing arrangements rather than becoming an extra task for the teacher. One of the advantages of using such a system is that it enables teachers to show progress which may be invisible using other systems.

Ampersand's progress

Ampersand began Nursery with no English. He had been cared for by his very affectionate but rather isolated grandmother. He was completely traumatised by his first weeks in school and needed all the patient understanding of the Nursery staff. Some parents wanted him to be removed from the class because he was disruptive and sometimes violent towards the other pupils. After a protracted settling-in period, Ampersand was able to enjoy his time in class and mix with the other children without tantrums or eruptions. By the end of the year, he could join in all the activities; he would speak a little in English and he could follow simple instructions. When he began Reception, his teacher was very anxious about his lack of English Language skills. However, recording his progress in a way which reflected the changes in his language behaviour showed that he had made appropriate progress in the Nursery.

It also showed what appropriate next steps could be targeted. Developing language behaviour takes place in all aspects of school life. Skills and knowledge are taught, not in isolation, but across all curriculum areas and in all activities. Ampersand's teacher would be looking next for evidence of his listening to stories, joining in with action songs and rhymes and sharing games with other children. Comma's teacher would be looking for times when he communicated with his peers and would have a target for a certain amount of speech from him each lesson, starting with short responses to closed factual questions asked directly of him, and moving on to more open-ended questions. One step forward for Comma would be to extend his short answers and ask him to repeat the full version. Both teachers would be looking for progress not just during lesson time but also during breaks and at the start and close of sessions. How Ampersand helps to tidy up and how Comma keeps up with his homework are just as significant as how their vocabularies increase in size.

Because of this, the teachers' EAL input is also significant in the design of class-room displays, the choice of resources, the nature of home–school communication, the organisation of trips and other activities. Teaching children with English as their second (or even third) language is 'holistic', i.e. it is about the whole pupil and the whole school. This is another of the key concepts of EAL provision.

Context

This brings us to what is probably the most frequently used word in any discussion of teaching EAL. 'Context', ironically, represents potentially dozens of different ideas at different times.

A very tricky word, context.

To experience just how tricky context can be, try the following:

1   What does this mean?
    'CHANGE TO STREET RUNNING WITHOUT STEPS MODE'

2   What do you understand by 'my computer'?

3   Describe a Sally.

4   What is a muffin?

5   Consider:
    a reformed meat
    b loose carrots

    c family butcher

    d a musical child

Answers

1 Look at it in context, then you may have more idea:

Figure 2.3

Still puzzled? As a key visual, this picture is insufficient. You need more context clues. You are not a tram driver so the picture is not helping you. Knowing the picture was taken in Manchester Victoria Station might help. Knowing that it was taken where the tram leaves the station to run on the street would be even better. You could probably make a much better guess now at what the words mean. You needed more contextual help than one picture, though.

2 In what context? In a discussion about things that cost too much and then get a bit boring, or as an icon on a monitor screen?

3 You might have your idea, but we were talking about bell-ringing. A Sally is the fluffy part of a bell rope, of course.

4 Where do you live and how old are you? It might be:

    a a round bread roll

    b a round flat soft bread roll

    c a round doughy object for toasting

    d a moist individual cake, especially with a lot of chocolate in it.

5 People can go a bit potty if they think about these for too long.

Returning to the classroom, we can consider how to assess a pupil's communication in context. The same pupil, with the same fluency in English, would perform differently in different contexts. Some of the meanings of 'context' in this case would be:

1. The situation the pupil is in

- Who is s/he communicating with? Peers, well known or unknown? Adults, known or unknown?
- Is the communication in what the pupil perceives as a safe or perhaps rather menacing situation?
- Has the pupil been able to 'rehearse' the communication, e.g. by working with a group or partner?
- Is the pupil familiar with communicating in this manner or is this culturally unfamiliar?

2. The content of the communication

- Is this familiar, in which case we can expect more in terms of both factual and syntactic accuracy, or is it new?
- Is it routine or may it spark some disagreement or criticism?
- Is it a statement of facts gathered from a source (along with much of the language needed to express it), or is it information generated by the pupil?
- Is it something the pupil has created, or something else personal, like an opinion or hypothesis?

3. The support available for meaning

- Has the pupil been able to gather enough information, through strategies like key visuals, use of the preferred language or other clues for meaning, or has lack of English restricted this?

4. The support for expression

- Has there been some form of scaffolding, such as a list of useful words and phrases, or help with organisation?
- Does the pupil have any means of supporting verbal communication, e.g. showing pictures or moving objects?

5. What is the pupil being judged on?

- Accuracy of content?
- Willingness to try?
- Accuracy of syntax?
- Appropriateness of expression?
- Adoption of technical vocabulary?
- Clarity?
- Length/amount of content?
- Pronunciation and intonation?

All the above looks like a rather forbidding list, but awareness of these variables will be an enormous help in assessing the pupil's progress and in planning how best to support learning and encourage English language development.

This brings us rather neatly to a summary of this key element of EAL provision:

SUMMARY

Teaching pupils with EAL requires a holistic approach to education in which close attention is paid to the context of learning and communication. This informs our assessment of progress, but it also has implications for the method and content of our teaching.

Exploring language and assessment

There is a big difference between the acquisition of social English and the mastery of the language of academic success. Imagine a foreign holiday. Within days, most talkative people will have learned some useful words – the names of things they buy frequently, for example, and perhaps a few polite phrases.

Imagine these holidaymakers extending their stay. After a few weeks, they will be greeting locals they meet regularly, and they will have found their way around the town so well that they will be using basic services like shops and buses with some success.

Within months, these chatty types will be having short exchanges with neighbours about, perhaps, the weather, their favourite food and sports teams, or the state of the geraniums on the balcony. Most of the chat will use language elements restricted to forms of very commonly used verbs: 'it is', 'they are not', 'we have', 'you like', and so on, coupled with an ever-growing supply of nouns representing objects they encounter most: 'cheese', 'football', 'money', and a limited number of the adjectives which they will need for so many transactions: 'big', 'right', 'happy', 'good', etc.

Within two years, they will still be making errors, but their accents will be very good. They will know many of the townspeople and will chat socially, talking about likes and dislikes, plans for little outings, who has been sick, who has a new car ... Most of their conversations will still be about what things are, what things are like and where things are. They will find it very easy, for example, to discuss bread and cakes while standing in the bakery with the baker. They will have learned all the customs and phrases relating to shopping, restaurants and transport. They will have a thorough knowledge of local attractions and will be able to assist other tourists. Anyone who meets them will remark how well they have adapted to a new life, how fluently they speak, how comfortable they must now feel.

They would, however, be quite wrong in assuming this. Put our long-term holidaymakers in the cinema, for example, and they will only cope with the most rudimentary dialogue and the simplest level of the plot – perhaps a car chase or two. Award-winning, intellectual masterpieces would be quite beyond them, even if they had worked as film critics at home. Give them an ailment more complex than a headache. How would they explain to the doctor if it were a stabbing pain, a shooting pain or a dull ache? They have spent their time in a quiet place for eighteen months; there have been no stabbings or shootings at all, and anyway, all those descriptions are metaphoric, so they do not translate easily.

We have not yet mentioned how the holidaymakers would fare when they decided to get a job. They could take orders in a café, or sell vegetables in a shop because they know all the words and the conventions associated with these situations. But they would not be very successful if they had to predict sales trends for writing paper, or write a column on social policy.

The holidaymakers can sound fluent and confident using the language of holidays because this is the life they know. It is also an easy language because it is about the straightforward, the concrete, and the here-and-now. Put into an unfamiliar situation, or a situation demanding complex and abstract language, they will sound like near beginners. Until they have an opportunity to be taught the deeper levels of their new language, they will never be able to communicate exactly what they feel, think, know and can do.

Transfer the same notions to real pupils, new to English, arriving in English schools. Such pupils, if they are chatty and confident types, if everything goes well for them, will show a similar, startlingly fast acquisition of the new language. They will learn the language and customs associated with the life of the school. They will use forms of common verbs: 'be', 'have', 'go' and 'do'. They will know the names of their classroom equipment, and the words their peers use for hobbies and socialisation, no matter how distasteful to adults. They will converse with relative ease on common topics, because they are familiar, or because they relate in an obvious way to the here-and-now. They can perform well on any assessments allowing them to use such skills. If their entry into English language learning coincided with their entry into the Foundation Stage, teachers unaccustomed to educating bilingual children could be forgiven for assuming that these children have a similar age-appropriate command of English to that of their monolingual peers. They do not. They have learned the English they have been *using*, no more and no less.

Similarly, teachers of older pupils are frequently so bemused by their varying performances in different situations that they assume there is some nefarious pretence at work. We remember one adolescent pupil who was particularly unhappy about having to move to England. She knew a little English and made it work for her as best she could, but a combination of dissatisfaction, hormones and cultural confusion rendered her speechless much of the time. Her teacher formed the belief that she secretly understood everything that was said and remained silent only through stubbornness. When she made the typical rocket-like progress of an intelligent bilingual pupil, he felt he had been right in his assumptions and that she had now dropped the pretence.

As well as language, there are socio-economic factors to consider. Thinking back to the holidaymakers, now late into their second year of seaside sun but still unable to function fully in unfamiliar situations, or to grasp complex or very creative uses of their new language. Assuming that they have urges to communicate beyond cocktail party chat and that they enjoy a good read, a thought-provoking film or a witty comedy, how can they satisfy these needs? Assuming they decide to work and have ambitions beyond selling hamburgers, who will employ them? The answer is simple: they will turn to each other, and develop a thriving English community for entertainment, the arts and mutual aid. The more timid or less able will spend most of their time within the shelter of such a community, while others will float in and out as they deem suitable. When English people living abroad form such a group, we describe it as an 'expatriate community', and it somehow calls up images of rather sophisticated types meeting for drinks on a pleasant veranda. This is very different from the common term used by many to describe just such a group comprising immigrants to England. We tend to call that a 'ghetto'. No clinking of glasses on the veranda here. 'Ghetto' carries with it a sense of poverty in every sense. It has a slightly judgemental aspect – 'those people really should have moved on from there by now, I expect it is just laziness!' We really should have moved on from finding it surprising when groups of people who share a common linguistic and cultural heritage band together because they understand each other much better.

Returning to the language issues, however, we have two points to consider:

- Bilingual pupils perform at different levels of fluency in different contexts.
- Bilingual pupils acquire social language quickly and easily, but may struggle with academic language.

The differences between the social and the academic are particularly marked in English, because it is a hybrid language. Most of us are familiar with the story that our words for animals and meat are different because, after the Norman Conquest the peasants raised the animals but then the lords and ladies ate the best bits. We still call the live animals by the Anglo-Saxon sounding 'hen', 'sheep' and 'cow' but we have on the menu French-influenced words like 'poultry', 'mutton' and 'beef'. The pattern goes far beyond this. In English, the vocabulary of our practical, informal everyday talk is full of remnants of the old Anglo-Saxon language while our technical, heightened or abstract formal communication shows a heavy Latin influence. Consider 'smell' and 'odour', 'illness' and 'malady'. You could make such comparisons all day and still not run out of words.

Many writers and thinkers have explored these and related areas, with different emphases at different times. Basil Bernstein's (1974) distinction between re-stricted and extended codes, for example, was concerned not just with elements of vocabulary and syntax but with the kinds of communication he believed various social groups regarded as appropriate. Trudgill (1975) explored tensions between Standard English syntax and working-class or dialect-speaking pupils.

For our purposes, the most helpful writer is probably Jim Cummins (1996, 2000), who distinguishes between Basic Interpersonal Communication Skills (BICS) and Cognitive Academic Language Proficiency (CALP). For a summary of the features of BICS and CALP see Fig. 3.1 overleaf.

Bilingual pupils, then, will be developing both BICS and CALP from day one. BICS will develop extremely quickly, so that an English language beginner can give an impression of fluency within a couple of years. CALP is not constantly reinforced by use in social life, so it develops much more slowly, and needs seeding, growing and nurturing in school. Academics are still wrangling over timescales for the acquisition of CALP, possibly because so many variables influence its development. Estimates range between 7 and 11 years.

Progress in EAL is assessed by observation of behaviour connected to communication, socialisation and learning in a variety of contexts. There are no pen and paper or scripted assessment tools, and nor should there be. Progress in EAL

BICS	CALP
Everyday vocabulary	Full range of vocabulary
Basic, simple syntax	Full range of structures, including complex forms such as third conditionals and passive voice
Meaning often made clear by external clues	Meaning dependent on interpretation of language
Spoken language, or language written like speech	Written language, or spoken language sounding like written language
Can be very informal	Always formal
Meaning can be greatly supported by gesture and tone of voice	Meaning not usually supported by gesture or tone of voice
Language used to narrate, describe, name, compare . . .	Language used to predict, evaluate, justify, persuade, hypothesise, infer . . .

Figure 3.1 BICS and CALP

is assessed in the playground, in the canteen, during Science, during PE, during History . . . We watch and we listen, noting responses to communication, whether as simple as making eye contact or as sophisticated as criticising a hypothesis. We note in what circumstances the pupil communicates and to what extent. Is she, perhaps, fluent in the card school but still grunting at the head teacher? Is he writing simple narrative accurately but not yet coping with description?

We gather our evidence, taken from all subject areas and all aspects of school life, and we use it to place the pupil on a developmental continuum. Good EAL assessment, then, needs to be:

- cross-curricular: about communication and study skills, not just about English as a subject;
- about the later stages of fluency as well as the early ones;
- performed in the normal contexts of the school day;
- about all language skills: listening with understanding, speaking communicatively, reading with understanding and writing effectively.

Once we have the evidence, we need to place the pupil somewhere on the continuum in order to assess if progress is being made and to plan for the best ways of moving on. In this publication, we are using the 7-Step system devised by the Northern Association of Support Services for Equality and Achievement (NASSEA). What follows is an introduction: a further explanation can be found in Chapter 4.

The NASSEA Steps are useful to us for a number of reasons. First, they can be interpreted at an age-appropriate level, so teachers at all Key Stages will be able to use them. Secondly, because they build on the QCA document *A Language in Common* (2000), they fit in with what may be the only system some teachers have met before.

The QCA document, being more focused on English as a National Curriculum subject, ends after four steps. These four steps provide two steps to reach National

Curriculum level 1. These are called steps 1 and 2. Next, level 1 itself is divided into two steps, called 'level 1 threshold' and 'level 1 secure'.

The NASSEA Steps system, adopted by many schools in the country, covers learning behaviour across the curriculum and concerns itself with the need pupils may have for various forms of support. This system ends at Step 7. It is reproduced (with kind permission from NASSEA) in the next chapter. A fuller explanation of the use and principles of this system is available from NASSEA in the inexpensive booklet entitled *EAL Assessment: Guidance on the NASSEA EAL Assessment System* (NASSEA 2001).

Observations about a pupil can be reviewed and compared to the descriptions of typical behaviour at each step. Pupils regularly operate in different steps for different skills. It is very common, for example, for listening /understanding skills to be in advance of writing skills. Pupils will also be more forthcoming in some situations than others, either because they feel more confident or because the demands of the occasion encourage it. The most accurate pictures of a pupil's language use will be gained from situations in which s/he is required to undertake some form of genuine communication within 'safe' circumstances. It is, of course, unlikely that anyone could accurately detail anything as complex as an individual's full language repertoire while continuing to perform those little tasks we call being a teacher and a human being. However, being 100 per cent accurate about sticking labels on pupils could not be described as the most important of our roles. What is more important is that we use the information we have as sensibly and as sensitively as we can to plan for the pupil.

The following chapter can be used in this way. It offers descriptions of typical behaviour observed at each step, along with suggestions for appropriate long- and short-term targets, with ideas for teaching strategies.

It can only be used properly, however, with this in mind:

SUMMARY

A key element of teaching pupils with EAL is that teachers understand the distinction between BICS and CALP, and that they plan in order to develop CALP in all subject areas.

Targets and teaching strategies

The Northern Association of Support Services for Equality and Achievement's (NASSEA) system for English as an Additional Language Assessment is based on the National Curriculum assessment system. Usually called the NASSEA Steps, this system has been introduced as a means of monitoring pupils, not only in the early stages of acquiring English, but also in the later stages. The first four steps are identical to those proposed by QCA. The later steps inform practice for teachers of pupils who have made more progress. The steps can inform target setting. This chapter uses the NASSEA Steps (reprinted here by kind permission from NASSEA) to describe how most pupils move forward in their acquisition of EAL and it gives our interpretation of how this may seem to a teacher and what actions we could suggest as appropriate to build on pupils' progress. The first four steps are copyright to QCA and are easily available from their website (www.qca.org.uk). The most straightforward way to get to the downloadable pdf file is to type 'A Language in Common' in the search box, then to press enter. From there, scroll down to EAL.pdf.

Acquiring an additional language necessitates the pupil developing language skills across four main areas:

- Active Listening.
- Speaking.
- Reading.
- Writing.

Because so many curriculum activities are geared to reading and writing, the essential listening comprehension and speaking skills are easily overlooked. For bilingual pupils, it is essential that activities and targets address all four language areas, especially active listening and speaking skills.

Target setting is dependent on the pupil's needs. Targets should reflect the rapid progress made by most EAL pupils. As progress is usually rapid, it is recommended that a number of short-term targets (between eight and ten) can be used as a checklist throughout one term.

It should be noted that pupils will probably not be at the same step for each skill. It is common, for example, for language learners to achieve a higher level in listening than in speaking.

Points to remember are:

- Make good use of class observations (how often the pupil interacts, and when and with whom).

- Collect evidence – what the pupil can do, what the pupil can say/understand.

- Be specific about any difficulty/concern.

- Plan what to do, set targets, and note when and how the targets will be achieved.

- Allow the pupil to work to the targets for a set length of time before revising them.

- Review progress.

- If in doubt seek advice from someone with EAL teaching expertise. This could be, for example, an LEA consultant or adviser, a contact from a website or an Ethnic Minority Achievement teacher.

The following pages contain suggestions for long-term aims and short-term targets, which should enable pupils to complete each step. All suggestions will need interpreting according to context. For example, '*to use print to convey meaning*' will have a very different meaning for staff in the Foundation Stage to that understood in Key Stage 4.

In order to use this chapter effectively, it is first necessary to establish a particular view of the curriculum (see Figure 4.1)

Figure 4.1 illustrates a wide view of the curriculum. A narrow view would contain only a body of knowledge and perhaps some associated skills. Techniques offered as suggestions for 'access to the curriculum' are generally concerned with this narrow view. The wider view is concerned with learning thinking skills and processes. To ensure that bilingual pupils have real access to the curriculum, we must enable them to have access to the cognitive aspects as well as the factual elements. Access strategies, therefore, need to be interpreted with this in mind.

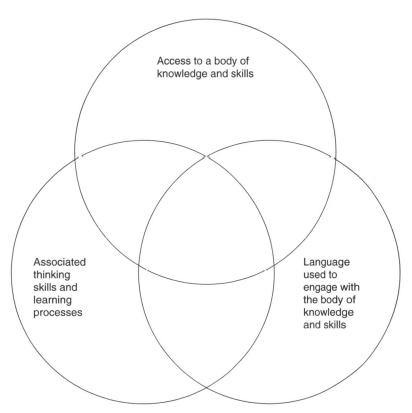

Figure 4.1   Venn diagram illustrating the interaction between Elements of the Curriculum

Teaching suggestions

There are some teaching suggestions which remain appropriate for learners at all stages of acquiring EAL. These represent the bedrock of EAL practice and change only in the degree of sophistication required as the pupil grows more fluent. Further exploration of these techniques can be found in other sections, but it is appropriate to list them briefly at this point:

1   The use of preferred languages. Concepts and ideas can be developed in any language. They do not necessarily have to be developed in English. This means that an appropriate role for parents might be to use preferred languages to explore and develop the concepts being learnt at school in English. This also means that pupils who share a common language should not be discouraged from using this in the classroom. Odd though it might sound, using preferred languages does facilitate English-language acquisition. For example, a pupil who has heard and understood a story will, on hearing the English version, start to pick up phrases and words which describe the events s/he remembers. This will also be true for older pupils in factual subjects.

2   The use of key visuals, i.e. facts and ideas conveyed through pictures, tables, diagrams, models, graphs, videos, photographs (the list is endless). Key visuals can communicate to pupils, or pupils can use them to indicate a depth of understanding beyond what can be expressed in language.

3   Collaborative group work, i.e. ways of organising the pupils so that they work together and, as part of the task they undertake, they have to communicate with each other and exchange information in a tightly structured way.

4   Transforming information from one mode into another, e.g. talking about a picture, then labelling it, then using the labels to fill in a table, then using the table as the basis for text.

5   Modelling. This can be done by adults or peers. Items to be modelled could include processes, grammatical patterns or usage. Modelling gives the bilingual pupil a template to work from.

A Step-by-step approach

Step 1: willing to communicate

In terms of spoken English, Step 1 has some parallels with the initial 12 months of first language acquisition. It is all about recognition and practice of sounds and words, and about the patterns of intonation, or 'tunes' of the language. Like a baby, new learners begin by manipulating and responding to whatever they experience. Unlike a baby, these new learners already have an extensive body of knowledge and skills which will inform these responses. When teachers recognise their pupils' prior learning, they can capitalise on this to increase attainment – linking new learning to established skills. For this reason, pupils should not normally take a whole 12 months to complete Step 1! How long they will take depends on factors such as age, situation and motivation. Again it should be stressed that pupils can operate in different steps for different skills; literacy skills, for example, tend to follow behind development of spoken language. An exception to this rule can be found in some older pupils who have learned English abroad and feel most confident with the written forms. Most pupils will make rapid progress.

(A full description of Steps 1, 2, 3 and 4 is available from www.qca.org.uk.)

To sum up Step 1, it is characterised by becoming willing to, then starting to, communicate. It is about learning the routines of the classroom and the school day. It covers the time when the pupil adjusts socially to the new environment and starts to become part of a new peer group. During this time, the new pupils will tune in to English sounds and intonation, building up a repertoire of useful words and phrases. They will also be familiarising themselves with the appearance of English print and the kinds of behaviour expected from them in connection with texts in school situations. As always, appropriate teaching content should be taken from the curriculum as taught to the whole class. However, it may be helpful to note that teachers have often found themselves spending time on the following items:

- greetings;
- numbers;
- classroom nouns, names of foodstuffs, clothing items, subjects;
- common classroom instructions;
- shapes and colours;
- simple adjectives such as big/small, hot/cold;
- simple prepositions such as in/under/next to;
- forms of the verbs 'be', 'go' and 'have';
- days, months and time;
- survival expressions such as 'Can I have a . . .?', 'I like . . . /I don't like . . .', 'Where's the . . .?', 'What's that?'

These facilitate the development of key vocabulary and expressions that will foster early independence in the classroom.

In order for pupils to complete Step 1, the following targets could be used.

Long-term aims

- To become successfully adjusted to the new environment, making some use of the facilities on offer, interacting appropriately with a peer group and starting to be independent in some areas.
- To access the curriculum via key visuals and preferred language/s.
- To acquire conversational English.
- To acquire listening comprehension skills.
- To acquire early literacy skills or to transfer existing skills to English.
- To use preferred language/s to develop EAL.

Short-term targets

- To settle into the school routine.

- To take the lead from peers and respond to 'buddies'.

- To follow simple routine class instructions, first supported by specific clues such as visual prompts, or by copying other pupils.

- To follow simple routine class instructions more independently.

- To respond to own name and greetings.

- To use non-verbal gestures to make him/herself understood.

- To echo words and expressions used in class.

- To listen actively for short bursts of time.

- To express basic needs using single words or short phrases.

- To learn some frequently used nouns associated with the classroom.

- To understand that English print reads from left to right and top to bottom.

- To respond to information in print.

- To find items such as the title, the writer's name, etc. from a book.

- To respond to pictures or diagrams appropriately.

- To use a library system or similar.

- To start copying or over-writing.

- To use print to convey meaning.

- To recognise names and familiar words in print.

- To identify initial sounds of familiar words.

- To know the letter names which make up spellings of familiar words.

- To write own name and some familiar words.

Teaching suggestions for Step 1

- The 'buddy system' often works well (see Chapter 5, p. 54).

- Always use visual support wherever possible – pictures, photographs, pictorial dictionaries, real objects, drawings, diagrams.

- Pictorial dictionaries are usually an excellent resource and many have accompanying vocabulary activity books.

- Face the pupil whenever you are talking to him/her and expect him/her to watch you carefully.

- Speak in a clear voice using straightforward sentences.

- Avoid rapid speech and figurative or idiomatic expressions.

- Make a point of speaking to the pupil every session, even though s/he may not appear to understand.

- Allow time for the pupil to process what you have said: repeat the sentence if this is unsuccessful; only re-phrase if this does not seem to be working.

- Include the pupil in class lessons right from the very first day – these allow him/her to acquire vital listening comprehension and speaking skills.

- Some pupils go through a 'silent period' as they tune into a new language; this should not cause anxiety. Continue to behave as if you expect the pupil to respond to you. Monitor language behaviour over time and seek advice if there has been no progress after a couple of months.

- Use some opportunities to extend his/her speech, by modelling the correct form.

- Gradually include him/her in class discussion by direct questioning. A good way forward is to give the information first, followed by a direct question. You will know if you have done this too early, or in the wrong situation, because you will get no response! Allow another pupil to answer – this will model the right language and behaviour. Give more time and try again.

- Oral blank filling (e.g. *'The compound was called . . .'*)

- Drafting and note-making in the preferred language.

- Provide differentiated written tasks such as:
  - labelling nouns on to a picture or diagram
  - transferring information from one medium to another (e.g. from a chart to a diagram, or vice-versa)
  - sequencing activities, putting labelled pictures in order or in categories
  - finding, then marking or copying words from a text
  - word searches.

- Using the pupil's first language in order to record work is particularly useful for older pupils where the purpose is to enable the pupil to write with more freedom and greater depth than s/he is currently able to do in English. In these circumstances it may not matter if the writing cannot be translated for the teacher.

- Reading activities are an excellent way of engaging bilingual pupils. Good books with high quality illustrations are an endless source of new vocabulary and discussion. Always introduce the book first, talk about the illustrations and check the pupil understands the vocabulary. There are any number of language development activities which can be done with well-illustrated books, including making labels and captions in English or the preferred language/s, or asking questions that necessitate one-word answers. Dual-text books are particularly useful, and many come with tapes. Certain picture books do appeal to older readers as well. Books can be sent home so the pupil can re-read passages, perhaps with family help. With younger pupils especially, do use the dual-text books with the whole class. This makes the story into a shared experience, which can be the basis of all kinds of activities.

- NB: phonic work has a very limited value at this stage and should be confined to looking at words already in the pupil's vocabulary, especially those associated with the current topic.

- Because of the cognitive load on these pupils, it is essential that teachers plan to include respite activities, connected to the current work of the classroom but which can be completed at a slower pace, allowing the pupil to consolidate what has been done already. Examples might include leafing through books rich in pictures and diagrams and some kinds of ICT work.

> ## MATERIALS
>
> Some teachers have found the following successful:
>
> Clicker (useful beyond this Step as well), Crick software.
>
> All My Words (can be used successfully with older pupils as the teacher controls the format), Crick software.
>
> Thinkin Things (very versatile), Iona Software.
>
> Eiki Card Readers and Language Masters
>
> 'Words for School' and 'Phrases for school', published in many languages, by Mantra Lingua.
>
> Lingua word processing software in a variety of languages.
>
> Milet Bilingual Visual Dictionaries.

Step 2: phrases and connections

There is some analogy between pupils at this stage and first language development between 12 and 24 months. We can expect learners to communicate on matters of immediate concern or practical matters using short phrases, but they show by their responses that their comprehension is in advance of their productive skills. They may become increasingly frustrated by the difficulties they experience in communicating their thoughts. However, these pupils will now be learning to use and produce simple texts, basing their learning on the age-appropriate skills they have already developed in their preferred languages.

(A full description of Steps 1, 2, 3 and 4 is available from www.qca.org.uk.)

Step 2 is characterised by the pupils gaining some confidence and independence, especially socially. They will still be making rapid progress and will appreciate feeling that they are included in the class and that their level of English is not confused with their level of ability. During this time, they will be transferring existing literacy skills to English and seeking out the grammatical patterns that will help them to put together words into meaningful strings. They will continue to build a vocabulary based on what they experience, and opportunities for fostering their acquisition of English should arise throughout the school day. Typical items arising during this time include:

- developing the noun phrase, i.e. moving from naming objects towards being able to say exactly what thing it was, what it was like and where it was;

- extending the number of verbs in the vocabulary (not being over-particular about getting the grammar right, but definitely knowing more words);

- developing adverbials of time such as 'next', 'then', 'for half an hour', 'until Tuesday';

- gaining control over agreement for singular and plural.

In order for pupils to complete Step 2, the following targets could be used.

Long-term aims

- To increase in confidence as a member of the class and to start interacting with the wider school community.
- To function independently in both routine and simple classroom activities.
- To acquire conversational English.
- To access the curriculum.
- To acquire basic literacy and numeracy skills in English.

Short-term targets

- To listen attentively and watch when people speak to him/her every lesson.
- To make responses during group work, either verbally or non-verbally.
- To follow the gist of a simple, context-embedded conversation and give short answers which are accurate in meaning.
- To listen attentively during carpet time/class lesson, responding to some questions, or making some contributions (supported by embedded context).
- To respond appropriately to class instructions given one at a time.
- To answer a direct, closed question every lesson.
- To make good use of visual support, including pictorial dictionaries.
- To sequence a series of pictures and comment appropriately.
- To be able to express simple matters using single words and phrases.
- To reproduce modelled talk using simple grammatical structures.
- To read ten words learnt in one curriculum area, using the context of a current unit of study as a source.
- To share and follow a simple text when read aloud, with support.
- To build a writing vocabulary of 25 content words, chosen from the pupil's experiences in and out of school.
- To use a bilingual dictionary (if literate in his/her preferred language) and maintain own word banks.
- To write an SVO (i.e. subject, verb, object) sentence with support every lesson.
- To recognise the different kinds of text they meet in school.
- To produce labels or captions that add meaning to visuals relating to familiar topics.
- To continue to build phonic skills using known words from the curriculum and school experiences.
- To begin to work out how to read and spell regular items.
- To continue to develop handwriting skills.
- To start to use handwriting as a tool for communication.

Teaching suggestions for Step 2

Many of the suggestions made for Step 1 can be developed further in Step 2.

- Always encourage the pupil to talk about the task he/she is about to engage in.

- Group work/pair work – plan group activities where the pupil will be an active participator. Structured collaborative activities are ideal for language development and benefit all pupils.

- Differentiated writing activities include:
  - sorting mixed sentences into categories, e.g. 'these are true, these are false', 'these are about the Victorians, these are about today . . .'
  - completing sentences
  - sequencing sentences
  - cloze procedure
  - finding one-word answers
  - using flash cards to create sentences.

- Ensure the pupil is placed in a group containing pupils who will act as good speech models for at least some of the day. Pupils learning through EAL should never be placed in lower groups all day solely because of language issues or unfamiliarity with the English culture or education system.

- It is important that the focus of any support is on developing listening comprehension and speech, using the curriculum as a source.

- Continue to use the buddy system and encourage other pupils to explain tasks/activities.

- Encourage the pupil to respond to simple questions using one-word answers or short phrases. Model answers first if necessary, and explain the words he/she does not know.

- Check the pupil understands simple classroom instructions.

- Use strong visual support wherever possible, including pictures, diagrams, charts and picture dictionaries.

- Expect the pupil to observe people carefully when they are speaking.

- Speak to the pupil every lesson. Give explanations slowly and clearly.

- Improve the pupil's sentence structure by reflecting his/her speech in extended form, e.g. just as 'Paper, Miss' can be rephrased as 'Can I have some paper, please?', so contributions such as 'float' can be remodelled as 'So you think it's going to float? I think it's going to float, too. Shall we see?' This technique is often used with young learners acquiring their first language and is very effective.

- Check the pupil's comprehension through direct questioning. Bilingual pupils tend to be good at sitting quietly and often miss essential information.

- Encourage one-word answers until the pupil progresses beyond this. If necessary start the answer, allowing the pupil to fill in odd words. Gradually extend speech to phrases and short sentences. Give the pupil part of a sentence and let him/her finish it.

- Praise the pupil's efforts. Remember that people in situations where they cannot understand what people are saying become very sensitive to body language, tone of voice and 'atmosphere', so reassurance is very important. They may even imagine slights or criticism where there has been none.

- Make sure the pupil is fully included as much as possible. Nobody learns a new language by being sent away from the place where people are using it purposefully.

- Share text which has good quality visual support. Always read the text to the pupil at this stage as they need to hear good role models of English. It serves little purpose in expecting the pupil to read aloud unsupported. The vocabulary will need to be explained and the text fully discussed before shared reading. Well-illustrated texts and dual-language texts are very helpful.

- Pupils at Step 2 find using semantics as reading cues rather difficult as they lack the necessary vocabulary. Some pupils develop excellent decoding skills. It should not be assumed that these pupils understand everything they read. Comprehension checks are therefore very important.

- Introduce key words from the main curriculum areas. Encourage the pupil to keep key word lists.

- Shared writing activities are ideal at this stage.

- Check written work with the pupil and re-read any corrections.

MATERIALS

The resources mentioned for Step 1 will continue to be useful. Wordbar, from Crick software, is also popular at this and later stages. It is rarely necessary to think of buying resources specifically for teaching pupils with EAL, apart from dual-language resources. It is more usual to choose class resources which have strong key visuals and which enable the teacher to deliver language-based lessons.

Step 3: really getting started

The English linguistic competence of pupils at Step 3 has some similarities with a native English speaker two or three years into language development; for example, pupils are moving towards connected, regular utterances although still of a limited nature. Like the native speaker, they will become more confident and fluent if given plenty of opportunities to converse and if more experienced users of English help them to find the grammatically regular forms they are seeking. If we constantly nag about the correctness of a communication before we listen to the content, they will become reticent and uncommunicative. Unlike the young native speaker, older pupils will already be experiencing differing levels of more sophisticated expression in another language, and will therefore not necessarily be learning linguistic concepts for the first time. Concepts already learned need only translating into the English expression. On the other hand, learning new concepts through English can be problematic and thought needs to be given to ways of imparting meaning which ensures conceptual development continues at an appropriate level.

(A full description of Steps 1, 2, 3 and 4 is available from www.qca.org.uk.)

Pupils completing Step 3 will really know their way around the classroom and the school. Depending on individual situations and personalities, they may seem confident and well-adjusted socially. This is the time when the pupil is starting to make an impact. As the pupils become more fluent and more confident, they will interact more freely and we get to know who was hiding under all that silence. Teachers often exclaim that their bilingual pupil is now 'like a different person'. In class, they are still struggling noticeably to understand anything unfamiliar or abstract, and their English speech is not yet developed enough to enable them to express ideas with clarity. These pupils are still very busy with learning the nuts and bolts of English – a process which carries an intellectual demand all of its own. Typically, teachers find these pupils need assistance with the verb phrase; with using appropriate tenses, for example, or building in appropriate adverbials. Pupils continue to need a good deal of visual support and vocabulary building.

In order for pupils to complete Step 3, the following targets could be used.

Long-term aims

- To begin to acquire listening comprehension and speaking skills in an academic context (i.e. to be able to compare, predict, explain and describe; see the Cummins Framework (p. 2) for a fuller explanation).

- To gain self-confidence, joining in class discussions and taking a full part in group work.

- To gain control of a range of grammatical structures.

- Independently, to produce short text with accuracy.

Short-term targets

- To listen attentively to a range of speakers and respond appropriately with support.

- To listen to class instructions and respond appropriately with support.

- To listen attentively to a class presentation and respond by answering simple, direct questions correctly with support.

- To listen with understanding and be able to re-tell familiar contents with factual accuracy.

- To begin to use context clues to establish the meaning of unfamiliar words.

- With support, to express an opinion clearly, if not with complete grammatical accuracy.

- To express and share ideas and facts relating to practical matters of immediate interest.

- To re-tell a short narrative or sequence of events in a familiar, supportive setting.

- To identify final and initial letter sounds in unfamiliar words.

- To follow short, simple written instructions.
- To read aloud simple sentences using familiar words in a supportive context.
- To comment on the content of a text on a familiar topic.
- To relate text to illustrations.
- To develop an understanding of rhyme.
- To extend vocabulary through the curriculum.
- To produce recognisable letters and words.
- To produce simple written sentences with some correct grammatical structures.

Teaching suggestions for Step 3

- Visual support is still essential, as this will help comprehension when new subjects are introduced. Use pictures, diagrams, charts, tables, bilingual dictionaries and picture dictionaries.
- Encourage the pupil to answer in class using phrases and short sentences, even though these may not be grammatically correct.
- Place bilingual pupils in groups where they will have access to good language role models as much as possible. Do not place pupils learning through EAL in low groups automatically because of language difficulties or unfamiliarity with the English education system. Be aware that these pupils should not be placed in sets or groups according to what they can produce on paper, as this will not be a true reflection of their ability.
- Pupils learning through EAL need the stimulation of a rich language environment as well as the opportunity to interact with both adults and peers.
- Aural comprehension usually develops faster than speech. Allow the pupil access to complex speech but accept simplified responses, or responses made through other media. NB: sometimes older pupils who have learned English in another country are more confident reading and writing than speaking and listening until they have adjusted to the local varieties of English.
- Check comprehension frequently by asking direct questions, for example, 'Tell me again what happened to the potassium', or 'Where did Henry meet Catherine?'
- Ensure that the pupil is fully involved in all curriculum areas and all activities, including class discussions.
- Read text to the pupil and discuss it. Be aware that many bilingual pupils develop excellent decoding skills but are unable to understand what they are reading. Build in purposeful interaction with the text.
- Check the pupil has the vocabulary needed for each topic. Make sure s/he has access to vocabulary lists. Pupils learning through EAL need support not just with subject-specific or technical vocabulary, but with many other semantic areas, including idiomatic expression.
- Give the pupil plenty of encouragement, especially for speaking. Confident pupils make faster progress; this has an enormous importance for language development. Pupils with a good self-image will feel more prepared to vocalise

and to take risks. Give correct language models and extend the pupil's speech without over-correcting. Respond to content before form.

- Expect rapid progress with reading and reading comprehension. Encourage re-reading at home.

- Where possible, give introductory sessions on books or texts to be studied. This allows the pupil to grasp what the text is all about and can make a lot of difference to progress. Some KS 1 and 2 texts are available in dual-language editions, which can be sent home so parents can prepare the pupil for the next book. Some of these are also available on tape.

- Differentiated writing tasks are essential. The pupil will benefit from scaffolding support, text modelling and the use of word lists and dictionaries.

- Continue to teach some phonics and handwriting skills within the context of other learning, using methods appropriate to the pupil's age and situation. Most bilingual pupils should acquire these skills rapidly. However, phonic skills need to be acquired and practised using content and activities derived from current classroom experiences. The pupil will be acquiring a great number of other language and literacy skills; phonics and handwriting do not necessarily take precedence. It would be counter-productive, for example, to withdraw bilingual pupils from part of the curriculum to teach them phonics in isolation from meaningful expression.

- Using sequencing cards is an ideal way to scaffold sentence production. Cards can be pictures, text or a combination of both. They can be fact or fiction and they can be used with any age group. Some commercial resources are available: 'Oxford Reading Tree' has a set in the teacher's handbook and the 'Card it' computer program (Crown House Publishing) makes designing attractive cards quick and easy.

MATERIALS

Now and at the following stages, we can recommend the packs designed and distributed by Nicholas Roberts Publications. These can be used at a variety of levels and for different age groups. They combine excellent visuals with highly scaffolded writing development, all within the context of the National Curriculum.

Step 4: The Big One

There is a huge difference between Steps 4 and 5. Therefore, expect pupils to spend longer here than on any earlier steps. During Step 4, pupils are reaching a point where they are beginning to sound like native speakers in familiar situations, especially socially. In more demanding situations, however, they may face problems of both comprehension and expression. Generally, they can still understand more than they can say. Early in Step 4, they are more concerned with content and meaning than with accuracy.

(A full description of Steps 1, 2, 3 and 4 is available from www.qca.org.uk.)

Completing Step 4 is about sharpening up, about developing regular syntax and about making a big stride forwards in reading. Typically, the pupil will be starting to use a larger variety of syntax items (not necessarily appropriately) and it would be unrealistic to suggest a list beyond the basic one referred to in the targets. A better idea would be to look at the content of the coming lessons and select a structure or a language function naturally springing from the topic or the activities. Then decide how you will highlight it and enable your pupil to practise it. Planning with a Cummins Framework is useful at any stage, but will certainly help clarify a teacher's thoughts as the pupil progresses into Step 4 and beyond.

In order for EAL pupils to complete Step 4, the following targets could be used. Again we stress that there is a considerable difference between Steps 4 and 5, so do expect this progression to take time.

Long-term aims

- To acquire understanding and fluency in spoken English at an academic level (see Cummins Framework for details).

- To access the National Curriculum using appropriate support or scaffolding for more complex or abstract ideas.

- To acquire English-speaking skills approaching those of his/her age group.

Short-term targets

- To listen to a series of instructions and respond appropriately every lesson.

- To follow class conversations and respond appropriately during the majority of lessons.

- To listen to and be able to pick out essential information during a class presentation with some accuracy, depending on the nature of the topic and the form of the presentation.

- To use the most common connectives, e.g. 'and', 'but', 'so', 'next', 'first', 'because', etc. correctly.

- To use the basic tenses accurately, e.g. the simple past and the 'going to' future.

- To use some adjectives and adverbs correctly, as appropriate within the context of the curriculum.

- To understand and use new vocabulary during all lessons.

- With support, to comment about text content with accuracy.

- To speak to adults and pupils in connected utterances.

- To produce handwriting acceptable within the age group.

- To use groups of phrases and statements to convey meaning in writing with some grammatical accuracy.

- To produce short pieces of text independently.

- To use scaffolding effectively to extend writing.

- To make some use of punctuation.

Teaching suggestions for Step 4

- Small group work where each individual pupil makes a contribution is ideal. Usually a bilingual pupil at this stage will join in a group task but may be unwilling to join in a whole-class discussion.

- Extend the pupil's length of conversation by two/three exchanges.

- Always check the pupil's comprehension through direct questions.

- Ask the pupil to explain the task they are carrying out.

- At this stage oral work is still extremely important. It also primes pupils for any following reading or writing tasks.

- Check the pupil has access to word banks, maintains his/her own word lists and uses a dictionary.

- Any additional support should focus on the introduction of any new text or topic the class will be studying. Most bilingual learners are able to function at a high cognitive level despite lacking the necessary skills in English.

- Set challenging tasks where support or scaffolding is available.

- Expect rapid progress with reading, especially if the pupil has literacy skills in their preferred language. Check the pupil's comprehension, as bilingual pupils often understand at a superficial level unless their attention is drawn to deeper levels of meaning. Draw them into a conversation about the text.

- Shared writing tasks are ideal as these involve all the language skills – listening comprehension, speaking, reading and writing. It can also be a way of extending and developing language.

- Linking any written task to the curriculum will have far better outcomes than giving the pupil language tasks that are unrelated to any areas of the curriculum.

- Ample scaffolding support can greatly enhance the quality of any EAL pupil's writing. EAL pupils benefit from support in structuring written work. They need to be encouraged to talk about and 'rehearse' any writing tasks.

- Paired reading schemes work well for pupils at Step 4 reading.

- In class, all kinds of text-marking and interactive reading strategies are appropriate. Use Directed Activities Related to Text (DART) and/or plan using Extending Interactions with Text (EXIT) ideas (as described in the Exeter Extending Literacy Project).

- Have the pupils listening, or watching out for specific pieces of information. Direct their attention by giving them listening tasks like 'spotting sheets' or 'clue sheets' to complete during lessons.

- Choose a grammatical target for a lesson and engineer the pupil's attention and production towards it.

- Primary school teachers can focus on language structures during sentence-level work in the Literacy Hour.

- At Key Stages 3 and 4, some pupils who have learned English before coming to the UK are more comfortable with paper-based activities than with speaking and listening. This is because they can use existing skills (e.g. consulting a dictionary) and can work at their own pace. Collaborative group work would support these pupils in developing their spoken English.

> ## MATERIALS
>
> For this and the following steps, these materials might be helpful:
>
> - 'Inspiration' from Inspiration Software. This tool for developing and recording thoughts can be used in many ways for bilingual and monolingual pupils. A free evaluation copy can be downloaded from www.inspiration.com.
>
> - 'Developing Tray', published by 2Simple software, for development of reading skills. This software can be used with any text, not just with the included poems, some of which may be culturally inappropriate for bilingual pupils.

Step 5: fluent?

Pupils who have reached Step 5 are growing closer in fluency to some of the monolingual English speakers in the class, but they still differ from their peers in many respects.

They will have a surface fluency which can mask their continuing difficulties with comprehension and expression. It would be easy to assume that these pupils are no longer in need of teaching sensitive to their language needs, but this would be a mistake. With the right support and appropriate challenges, these pupils will achieve a high standard. On the other hand, some pupils may be alarmed by their continued struggle and develop strategies for avoiding situations which they fear could expose an inadequacy. They may limit themselves to 'safe' options, or become over-reliant on friendly assistance from peers or adult support. Certain pupils may choose to hide their anxieties by becoming difficult to teach in some way.

Step 5 can be described as follows.

> ### 1. Listening and Understanding
> Pupils can understand most conversations when the subject of conversation is more concrete than abstract and where there are few figurative and idiomatic expressions.
>
> ### 2. Speaking
> Pupils begin to engage in a dialogue or conversation in an academic context. In developing and explaining their ideas they speak clearly and use a growing vocabulary.
>
> ### 3. Reading
> Pupils use more than one strategy, such as phonic, graphic and syntactic and contextual, in reading unfamiliar words and extracting information from a variety of texts. From Key Stage 2 onwards reading has typically begun to be a tool for learning rather than a process which is an end in itself.
>
> ### 4. Writing
> Pupils are able to produce written outcomes using a range of appropriate grammatical structures, when given scaffolding support such as frameworks and a specific focus on the linguistic requirements of different kinds of writing. Pupils' production is more limited when they receive no such support.
>
> Pupils are beginning to understand that different contexts require different forms of expression and they will be attempting to respond to this understanding in their writing.

Step 5 is about communication becoming wider and deeper, especially in terms of using or producing text. It is about enriching vocabulary and learning how ideas can be arranged or explored in logical sequences. At Step 5, pupils can achieve high standards if scaffolding is given, but will dip markedly where it is not.

At this stage, teachers typically find their pupils able to function at an advanced level in the here-and-now or practical spheres of interest. Input for language development is often about extension: about adding to the range of adjectival and adverbial expressions in the pupils' repertoires, about exploring shades of meaning as illustrated by, for example, changing a verb from 'mix' to 'beat'. Grammatical input may be associated with advanced structures such as the passive voice, or third conditionals.

In order for EAL pupils to complete Step 5, the following targets could be used.

Long-term aims

- To acquire higher-order listening comprehension skills.
- To improve fluency and accuracy of speech in order to express higher levels of thinking.
- To access the National Curriculum, with little support.
- To acquire age-appropriate literacy skills.
- To work independently in class.

Short-term targets

- To understand and participate in conversation with adults and peers.
- To grasp essential information from a class discussion/lesson on mostly concrete or practical matters, without support.
- To understand the gist of a class lesson when little visual support is used.
- To be able to explain his/her own ideas using regular sentence structures.
- To engage in and maintain an individual conversation with an adult on an academic level, e.g. expressing an opinion, explaining a prediction.
- To be able to review a story, book or other text, stating the main events or points.
- To be able to summarise a text accurately.
- To use syntax cues to interpret text.
- To use contextual cues to interpret text.
- To use phonic cues for decoding.
- To re-tell story content with accuracy and fluency.
- To read with fluency, using mostly correct intonation.
- To interrogate text for facts.
- To begin to understand figurative expressions in English.
- To plan a story/piece of written work.
- To write, with some scaffolding, sequentially, giving a clear account of a familiar topic.
- To write using short paragraphs with little support.

- To write in a variety of contexts or genres, with support.
- To use a variety of grammatical structures, with support.
- To write in sentences using a variety of correct grammatical structures.
- To write more complex sentences using a variety of connectives.

Teaching suggestions for Step 5

- The EAL pupil is acquiring both conversational and academic English skills simultaneously, therefore teachers need to be aware of the language demands of the classroom and take care not to confuse conversational fluency with the ability to manipulate and comprehend formal or complex language.
- As the EAL pupil will still need to make progress in English as well as in subject areas, make sure s/he has access to more difficult and challenging language experiences across the curriculum.
- Use any support available for discussing text to be studied in class before the event.
- Check the pupil's comprehension frequently by involving him/her in discussion.
- Ask subtle questions that need pupils to think about what they have heard or read; work on inference.
- Collaborative group work where each member is expected to contribute and information is moved from one medium to another is ideal for any bilingual learner.
- The pupil should be encouraged to contribute in class at an academic level, e.g. by expressing an opinion about a book, re-telling text content, or suggesting options.
- Pupils will benefit from their spoken language being extended and developed. They still need good role models at this stage.
- Be aware that the EAL pupil is still acquiring vocabulary and will need access to dictionaries, including bilingual ones.
- As EAL pupils are developing sentence structures, include linguistic work on conditionals, tenses, etc., or use subject texts to illustrate how these are used.
- Make extensive use of writing frameworks and modelled writing.
- Provide access to good quality text, as role models will help all bilingual learners.
- Re-reading and checking a piece of written work with the pupil is beneficial. Examples of how language can be developed can be talked through immediately in context.
- Directed Activities Related to Text are ideal at this stage.

It is very easily assumed that once a bilingual pupil has conversational skills, they are 'fine'. Whilst it takes up to two years for an EAL pupil to acquire conversational skills, it takes much longer to acquire the full range of speech and literacy skills in order to operate at an academic level, e.g. to evaluate, predict, justify, hypothesise or argue a case. It is specific targeted support at this advanced level that can make such a difference to the attainment of an EAL pupil.

Bilingual learners respond well to being challenged, but, because they are carrying a cognitive load interpreting English at the same time, they need support which acts as 'pegs to hang their thinking on' while they process the language. Such support enables them to access the full range of lesson content without losing the thread while they manipulate the language elements. Techniques which enable this to happen include:

- sorting and ranking;
- concept mapping;
- brain storming;
- comparison charts;
- certain software (e.g. 'Inspiration');
- story boarding.

Step 6: the invisible bilingual

The pupil is now very much like the monolingual members of the class, but with some important differences. When these pupils reach a plateau in their progress, it is likely that it is because of the language demands of the subject or topic. It may have nothing to do with ability or motivation. To guard against underachievement, it is extremely important that these pupils continue to have appropriate targets set and that their teachers continue to be aware of their status as developing bilingual learners.

Step 6 can be described as follows.

---

1. Listening and Understanding
Pupils can participate as active speakers and listeners in group tasks. They understand most social and academic school interactions delivered at normal speed.

2. Speaking
Pupils use language appropriately across the curriculum for different academic purposes (e.g. explaining) – some minor errors may still be evident. They are able to use more complex sentences.

3. Reading
Pupils understand many culturally embedded references and idioms, but may still require explanations. From Key Stage 2 onwards pupils can read a range of complex texts, starting to go beyond the literal by using some higher-order reading skills such as inference, deduction and hypothesis.

4. Writing
Pupils can produce appropriately structured and generally accurate work in a variety of familiar academic contexts with few errors and without support. They will still require support to develop the organisational skills and appropriate linguistic forms for new contexts.

Step 6 is about becoming independent. It is about moving beyond the literal into competency in figurative and/or idiomatic English. It is about an extension into a richer vocabulary and accuracy of expression. As pupils move through Step 6, they will require less and less contextual support until, at Step 7, they will be able to operate at high levels without any support at all. Typically, pupils at Step 6 appear very fluent when the topic or task is familiar, but they need careful introduction to new topics, or structured support before they can express themselves in new ways.

In order for EAL pupils to complete Step 6, the following targets could be used.

Long-term aims
- To access the National Curriculum in full.
- To have good comprehension skills at an inferential level.
- To be a fluent speaker of English at an academic level.
- To be an independent learner.

Short-term targets
- To understand idiomatic speech.
- To recall the key points of a class presentation; stating facts with appropriate vocabulary and mostly accurate syntax.
- To use reading strategies effectively and apply them when reading unfamiliar words.
- To fully understand class presentations delivered at normal speed.
- To be an active listener, including asking for clarification when necessary.
- To understand speech and text at an inferential level.
- To make use of word lists and dictionaries independently.
- To speak using complex sentence structures, using conjunctions, adverbs, adjectives and the full range of English verb forms at an age-appropriate level.
- To read text for information.
- To read age-appropriate text with understanding.
- To be a confident participating class member.
- To check/proof and re-draft own work.
- To use higher-order reading skills of inference, deduction and hypothesis.
- To work on a range of complex texts, with support.
- To produce appropriately structured writing in a range of genres and contexts.
- To produce writing that is grammatically accurate, within a supportive setting.
- To understand most cultural references shared by the age group.
- To develop an extensive range of expressions.

Teaching suggestions for Step 6

Strategies appropriate for bilingual learners are always likely to aid their monolingual classmates, but particularly so at Step 6, where English language acquisition and learning subject-specific language are progressing closely together.

- Bilingual pupils should be placed in groups where they will be presented with challenging work. Language development opportunities can be found in all curriculum areas.

- Ensure there is an opportunity for the pupil to learn or to have explained any cultural references which may hinder them.

- Step 6 indicates the pupil is likely to be be working within levels 3 and 4 of National Curriculum English at KS 2. At KS 3 the pupil is likely to be entering level 5.

- A pupil may need some additional support to overcome grammatical errors. Verb tenses can still be a problem for some pupils. Any individual attention can be usefully focused in this area.

- Discuss use of idiom and figurative language.

- Continue to use Directed Activities Related to Text.

- Give mentoring-style support to aid organisational skills.

- Use of glossaries and word lists continues to be appropriate.

- Paired drafting.

- Graphic organisers, i.e. ways of using visuals to support thinking processes.

- Oral 'rehearsal' of written work.

- Deconstructing and reconstructing texts.

- Modelling writing and reading processes.

Step 7: independence

Step 7 indicates that the pupils no longer need to be assessed for EAL acquisition. They continue, however, to enjoy the cognitive and social benefits of bilingualism, while remaining, like their monolingual classmates, in need of teaching sensitive to the linguistic demands of the curriculum.

At this stage there is an expectation that EAL pupils have the full range of skills across all four main language areas, in order to fully participate within the National Curriculum and be fairly assessed using only the National Curriculum for English.

CHAPTER 5

Preparing for an EAL beginner

The greatest understatement in this book:

> The arrival of a pupil new to English, or with very limited English (we will call them beginners) can cause quite a stir in schools where this is an uncommon experience.

The most surprising statement in this book:

> Beginners are easy to accommodate because they have specific, easily understood needs.

The most unpopular statement in this book:

> Accommodating a beginner takes preparation, organisation, efficient communication and the support of the school's management.

The most popular statement in this book:

> Beginners do not need a teacher to design or adapt a whole syllabus just for them. Nor should any one teacher or group of teachers be expected to bring a beginner to full fluency in one short year.

Perhaps the above needs explanation. Understandably, school staff will be anxious when a beginner arrives, especially if they have had little experience of this and there are no EAL workers to advise or support them. Much of this anxiety, however, comes from looking at the event the wrong way round. If the teacher asks: 'How can he get a level 3 in two months?' or 'How will she complete her assignments?' then the answer to both questions could be 'Maybe not at all'. This is where the stress comes in, for both teacher and pupil. Of course, some of these pupils will achieve higher levels than one could at first imagine, but right now we are just at the beginning.

Looking at the event the right way round reduces stress for everyone and makes sound educational sense. We should start, like we always do, with the needs of the pupil. In the 1950s, Abraham Maslow developed a way of looking at human needs (Maslow 1987). According to him, the desire to use one's talents and to perform well is conditional upon the satisfaction of other, more basic needs. Therefore, our pupils will only be able to engage with what we provide for their education if their more basic needs are met.

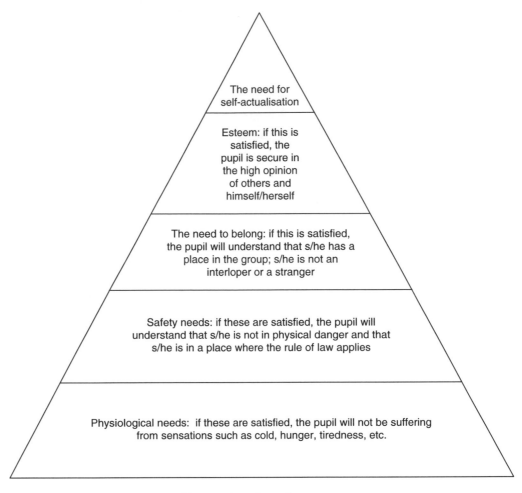

Figure 5.1 Maslow's original hierarchy of needs

Looking at Maslow's hierarchy in terms of what a pupil new to a school may need, we can devise some starting points.

To feel physically comfortable, the pupil will need:

- the correct equipment and clothing;
- knowledge of the best route to and from school;
- an understanding of the meals, drinks and snacks systems operating in the school;
- familiarity with the kinds of food available;
- some knowledge of when s/he is allowed time to relax, visit the toilet, walk around, etc.

To feel safe, the pupil will need:

- to experience fairness and justice in operation in the classroom;
- to experience fairness and justice in operation around the school generally;
- some understanding of the school rules.

The next two sections of the hierarchy are especially relevant to teachers of pupils who are new to the country or who are members of an ethnic minority group. Maslow has a strong message about the effects of pupil mobility:

> The destructive effects on children of moving too often; of disorientation; of the general over mobility that is forced by industrialisation; of being without roots or of despising one's roots, one's origins, one's group; of being torn from one's home and family, friends and neighbours; of being a transient or a newcomer rather than a native.
>
> (Maslow 1987: 20)

Maslow disapproved of mobility because of the damage he perceived it caused. He was writing in other times, however. In our times, mobility is a long-established reality bringing both advantages and disadvantages. We are interested here in the phrase 'of despising one's roots'. It may strike home to many. In the past, our education system was often rightly accused of forcing middle-class mores down the throats of working-class children. Consider this memory from one of our contributors:

> 'I can still remember the endless puzzle generated by "Domestic Science", involving as it did complex rules about table setting and intricate business about where you peeled the potatoes and how you disposed of the skin. Cooking for nine at home, on the other hand, I found simple enough.'

How much more alienated would her teenage self have been if there had been no other working-class girls there? If all the dishes and ingredients had been unfamiliar? If the only references to her kind of diet described it as either exotic or insufficient? If, when she set about making a shepherd's pie, the other pupils had felt free to comment frankly on how it smelt and how they did not fancy it at all, thanks? If the teacher had expressed concern when, after a couple of years she persisted in thinking a sponge cake was a nice idea for Sunday tea?

Pupils faced with images of a foreign culture all day long, coupled with subtle messages that there is something strange or wrong with the way they eat, dress, think and talk, will do one of two things. They will either retreat, feeling inferior or unwanted, or they will attack, feeling angry or under threat. Our aim is to keep all kinds of warfare out of the classroom.

There are plenty of sources of good advice about cultural sensitivity. As this book is largely about language, we pause here only to assert the huge importance of these issues, and to warn readers that this is a complex area, with causes and effects which are often subtle, perhaps even invisible to members of dominant heritage groups. It is not something one can easily figure out just using common sense.

The next two sections of Maslow's hierarchy, then, are bound up with feelings. To meet the needs of pupils from ethnic minorities and minority heritages, teachers need to be conscious of how the dominant heritage can unintentionally suppress achievement and well-being.

To feel a sense of belonging, the pupil will need:

- to be assured that s/he is welcome from the first footstep over the threshold, in as many ways as possible;

- to be included in the class from the first morning, in every sense of the word. Beginners are usually very sensitive to physical clues. If they have not got a proper seat at a table, if they have not got the same colour book as the others, if they have not got a peg or a locker, all this will be translated into a feeling of not belonging or of being unwelcome, which may take weeks or months to dispel;

- to be grouped sensitively and appropriately, either in mixed ability groups or with pupils who are good language models, certainly not with pupils who have learning difficulties;

- to experience displays and resources which include references to what is familiar to him/her.

To feel a sense of esteem, the pupil will need:

- evidence that his/her existing skills, languages and knowledge have a place in the new environment;

- familiar contexts in which to demonstrate existing skills;

- praise for achievements in all his/her spheres of activity, including those related to languages and activities not shared by the rest of the class;

- recognition that their task of operating in an unfamiliar environment in an unfamiliar language carries an intellectual load in itself, before the pupil begins to engage in lesson content;

- opportunities for success.

Looking at these starting points, we can see that some of them are more demanding than others. Some are outside the control of the individual teacher – it is not easy to keep a pupil comfortably warm and fed in a damp and draughty building where the dinners are not all they should be, for example. Nor is it always possible to ensure feelings of safety and belonging in a large institution such as a secondary school. As teachers, our best course of action is to deal thoroughly with that which we can control, and look for opportunities to exert some influence on the rest. How many school development plans include some kind of training in equal opportunities issues for welfare staff? Suggesting such an initiative is one small exertion which could result in a large pay-off.

Most of the more demanding needs can be met with a little preparation and organisation, although not all the work is the province of a class teacher. The active support of management and clerical staff is vital. It is also a very good idea to make sure you know what support is available for ethnic minority achievement in your local area. You need to hear this straight from the horse's mouth. Do not assume there is nothing, and do not listen to anyone who can only tell you what the situation was ten, five or even two years ago. Such organisations face frequent change, and people not on the spot may not have up-to-date information. One of us was once told by a council worker that she no longer existed, which she felt was rather premature. This council worker could easily have told any teacher with a query the same thing. Make good use of the internet to uncover structures which may be supportive of your pupil's needs. At the very least, you should be able to access a little advice.

The next section follows an imaginary pupil through an admissions procedure, pointing out the opportunities for preparation and planning. In this case, we are discussing beginners, i.e. pupils new to English. Parts of this procedure would also, however, be appropriate for more fluent pupils arriving from other schools or from abroad.

Bilingual mid-term admissions

1. Mr and Mrs Gerund make an appointment to see the head teacher of Future Perfect School with a view to enrolling their son, Participle.

The head teacher's secretary or clerical support notes what language the family uses for speech. If the parents are not confident users of English, they are asked if they can bring along an interpreter. If they cannot do this, the school will need to find one. This may be possible through local community links, through an agency or with the help of the local authority. The school may have to pay for this, but it will pay for itself several times over in better relationships, faster induction, more appropriate teaching and a great deal of saved time.

2. Mr and Mrs Gerund meet the head teacher.

This meeting will take a little longer than most admissions meetings. Use time now in order to save time later. The form overleaf is intended to guide the conversation, rather than to be filled in by the family before the meeting. It facilitates gathering the kind of information which will be useful in planning for the pupil. This version has been useful in some schools and can be adapted for your school's age range and local conditions.

In a conventional admissions meeting, crucial information is easily overlooked: if you are going to build on a pupil's previous knowledge and existing skills, you need to know about them. Existing admissions forms, while requiring basic information concerning ethnicity for statistical purposes, do not provide the staff with the information needed to take on board the previous education and existing skills of the pupil. Assuming the teaching and learning styles are similar to those of your school, or that the curriculum covered is similar, would be a naive mistake. It is always wise to ask.

Some school arrangements may be unfamiliar to parents who have been accustomed to another education system. Topics which may benefit from an airing include:

- How school and parents normally communicate and what is asked of parents.
- Homework and how parents are asked to support it.
- How parents can best support learning in general.
- Trips and visits: their value and safety arrangements.
- Parties or other celebrations: what happens and what they are for.
- Clubs and big projects such as class/school productions: who can join and how they benefit the pupils.
- Parent consultation meetings.

Admissions form

Educational details:

1 Previous schooling since age 5, including schools outside UK:

2 Length of time in last school:

3 If last school was outside UK, what subjects were studied? What can we gather about the syllabus to help us understand what general knowledge the pupil already has?

4 Any standards reached, grades awarded or qualifications achieved?

5 What has been the language of instruction for most of this pupil's schooling?

6 What were the pupil's favourite or best subjects?

7 Details of prolonged breaks in education or extended holidays within the last few years:

Languages used:

It is important to make sure the parents understand that you are not attaching any value judgements to which languages they use in the home. Some institutions mistakenly demote certain languages to an inferior status, either accidentally or through ignorance. Parents who have had experience of this in the past may have been made to feel that they are doing something wrong, or that they need to conceal the truth from you. Make sure they realise that conversing solely in English would be educationally and socially inappropriate for their child. Try to ensure that they tell you the truth – not what they suspect you want to hear, or what they suspect would be polite to say. Nobody promised this bit would be easy. Take your time.

1 What languages are spoken in the home? (This includes sibling–sibling, children–parents and children–grandparents. Some families develop a complex pattern, with each language serving a distinct purpose.)

2 How confident is the pupil in his/her different languages?

3 Have you any indications of how well the pupil expresses himself/herself in these languages?

4 Have you any indications of how sophisticated the pupil's understanding is in these languages? Are there any situations in which s/he can communicate particularly well, or in which s/he obviously struggles?

5 What languages are books, letters and newspapers, etc. in?

6 What languages are films, radio stations, etc. in?

7 What languages does the pupil read, and how well?

8 What languages does the pupil write, and how well?

9 Is the pupil attending any supplementary school for languages? Will the school be informed of the pupil's achievements?

10 Does the pupil own a bilingual dictionary which can be brought to school daily? Has s/he had enough practice and help to use it efficiently, or will s/he need some help at the start? Could anyone in the family do some coaching?

Medical information:

1   What inoculations has the pupil had? Are any missing?

2   When was the last eye test? Results?

3   When was the last hearing test? Results?

4   Does the family know how to organise all of the above? Can all medical matters be settled before the pupil starts school? What advice or support might the family need?

Religious information:

1   What religion does the pupil follow?

2   Are there any special requirements, e.g. diet? Restrictions? Observances? Festival dates? (Pupils are allowed time away from school for religious observance.)

3   Which language is used for religious purposes?

4   Does the pupil attend religion classes outside school time? How many hours per week? Will the school be informed of the pupil's achievements at religion classes?

3. There is a short breathing space.
   During this time, Mr and Mrs Gerund:

- Prepare school uniform, etc., having had the benefit of a thorough explanation of what is necessary.

- Ensure Participle has had health checks and is not starting a new school with hearing loss or blurred vision.

- Coach Participle in some useful skills.

During this time, the following happens at Future Perfect:

- Information is communicated to all staff. Participle is a beginner and may require a lot of help from teaching and non-teaching staff during the early weeks. He can be expected to make very fast progress, but teachers will need to be aware of his language needs right up to the end of his time at Future Perfect.

- Grouping is organised. The best place for Participle will be found in mixed-ability groups as these should contain enough levels of differentiation and enough use of multi-sensory teaching. Failing that, a mid- to high-ability group, will offer Participle articulate language models. A low-ability group, while easy for support and organisation purposes, only confuses lack of English with poor learning ability. It gives negative messages about Participle and leads to low expectations and self-esteem. If Participle has to be in a low-ability group, it must be for a limited length of time and with very clear targets and objectives which are reviewed frequently. If such a group constantly practises basic literacy skills out of any meaningful context, it will certainly delay Participle's development. If such a group concentrates on conversation skills and meaningful work supported by key visuals, it may be a suitable experience for a short time.

- Staff who will be teaching Participle can acquire suitable materials, approach appropriate bodies for advice and have a little time to plan how they will include him in lessons.

- One, two or all three of these specific initiatives can be organised: a 'panic file', a 'buddy' and an interpreter.

The panic file (KS 2, 3 and 4)

This enjoyably named strategy is a simple idea for reducing stress on both pupil and teacher during the early weeks. Whenever the pupil has reached a point at which the lesson has gone far beyond his/her ken and there is nothing to be done to salvage the next half-hour, the panic file contains useful activities requiring minimal English proficiency and which can be completed with little or no support. The pupil can complete these activities, thus avoiding the embarrassment and frustration of inactivity, and the teacher can continue teaching the rest of the class.

HEALTH WARNING
This is not an alternative curriculum for pupils with EAL. It is always preferable that teachers differentiate and plan for their new bilingual pupils. The panic file is a way of admitting that, just once or twice a day, for a little while, this may not always be possible.

How to organise a panic file

Somebody needs to have responsibility for this. Like most facilities for beginners, the difficult work is in the organisation. This is most complex in secondary schools, where it may not be obvious who should take responsibility. Management support is important here. Whoever does take it on, has these tasks to perform:

- Gather appropriate materials. Ask all the staff for anything they might have which fits the bill. Tap into your local support systems for ideas and examples. Some teachers have found the 'home help' style books available at newsagents and bookshops helpful. The *Oxford Junior Workbooks*, first published in the 1970s, are an example of this, if you are lucky enough to find some tucked away.

- Give the pupil ownership of the file. S/he will decide when to use it.

- Make sure there is a regular time available for marking and re-filling the file, preferably with the pupil present so you can give praise for what is completed and guidance for the new tasks.

- Have ideas ready for obvious and tangible praise – stickers, certificates, etc., whatever is currently used in your school. Remember that beginners need success and reassurance.

Suitable content

This depends on the nature of the school and the age of the pupil, but the following suggestions may be helpful:

- Use labelled pictures to enable the pupil to recognise nouns, then give practice at using these nouns in tasks requiring the pupil to sort, match and label.

- Use vocabulary relating to school subjects or school equipment.

- Set up a card reader with a stock of curriculum-related cards.

- Give practice at appropriate skills for the year group concerned, e.g. making a graph, copying a sketch map, handwriting practice, drawing a diagram.

- Set up a vocabulary book or homemade personal dictionary and encourage the pupil to spend panic time revising new vocabulary.

- Include a dual-text reader, or a grown-up-looking book in the pupil's own language.

- Using your knowledge of the pupil's previous education, include some reference to topics s/he will find familiar.

- When making your own worksheets, use the same format each time, so that the pupil quickly becomes familiar with some instructions and can access the work with minimal support. Suitable examples might include: 'tick the true statements', 'match the words to the pictures', 'circle the odd one out', 'put these in order', 'label the diagram', 'draw a . . .' 'underline all the . . .'

- Most beginners cope with simply expressed number work before they can access other curriculum areas (although this does depend on how number work is written in the preferred language). It is worth capitalising on this as a row of ticks does wonders for self-esteem.

- Some computer programs lend themselves to panic moments. 'All My Words' is a good example of this. Although intended for quite young children, this can be made attractive to older pupils by entering the curriculum-related words, phrases and sentences on a plain background (this is not at all difficult). 'Thinkin' Things' is another such program, and is useful for pupils much older than is suggested in the catalogue.

Buddy systems (KS 1, 2, 3 and 4)

This kind of peer support is hugely popular in a variety of settings, but is probably most useful in high schools. The most basic version involves one already-settled pupil taking some responsibility for the induction and welfare of a new pupil for the first few weeks. Sometimes it is possible to pair up pupils who share a common language, but this is not essential for the system to work. People of a similar age will manage to communicate without a common language much more easily than those of different ages, and this is particularly noticeable in the young.

It is also more appropriate for pupils to perform this task than for adults to attempt it. Apart from the obvious problems of timetabling adult support, think how difficult an adult would find the transmission of the following esoteric information:

- Who uses which set of toilets and when – how to avoid nasty incidents in this danger zone.
- Which parts of the grounds or buildings are safe and sheltered during break.
- Who is approachable, and who is not.
- The current changing-room etiquette.

The above is in addition to such adult-centred information as the use of the library and directions around the school, but is probably of more urgent importance to the pupil. Other tasks well served by this system include:

- The use of lockers or other storage facilities.
- Start and end of lesson routines (often still different for each teacher, even in schools where they are meant to be the same).
- Modelling the use of planners, journals or notebooks.
- Explaining the new pupil's silence to random adults or pupils not acquainted with the situation.
- Being a guide around the building.
- Being an emotional prop.
- Dinnertime routines and choices.

This list is not exhaustive. There are, in fact, so many jobs that a buddy can do that some schools having regular mid-term admissions organise a whole team of buddies on a businesslike contract. For an explanation of how this can work, we refer you to Claire Edmunds, of Goldsmiths' College, London University. One of the many benefits of organising the system this way is that it reduces the risk of existing friendship groups becoming disrupted. Under a contract system there can be no confusion over whether the teacher has asked the pair to become friends for ever; each buddy is simply working a shift for part of the day and not promising an extended involvement. Any longer-term friendship can develop naturally, like other school friendships.

However many buddies a teacher finds it right to mobilise, it would be wise to consider the following points:

- Make sure the buddy understands what is and what is not his/her responsibility. Stress for the buddy comes with taking on too much; stress for the new pupil comes with the buddy taking on too little.

- Set a time limit to the arrangement.

- Make time to check on progress frequently.

- Make sure there is some kudos attached to buddy work, either by rewards or public praise.

Buddy myths de-bunked

Some teachers express reservations about organising buddies for the following, entirely mistaken, reasons:

1. 'Settled bilingual pupils will not make progress if they are looking after a newcomer' This is not the case. All teachers are aware that the best way to understand something thoroughly is to explain it to another person. A settled bilingual pupil gains great confidence and self-esteem from being trusted to show someone else the ropes.

Oxymoron arrived from Bangladesh late in Year 7, speaking Sylhetti and a little English. After about six months, two other Sylhetti speakers arrived and were placed in her form. By Year 9 all three girls were speaking good social English and Oxymoron had made twice the usual rate of progress. Why? Because she had been the leader of the group, taking responsibility to listen extra carefully in case the others needed help. She grew very confident and communicative with both pupils and adults. Oddly enough, despite her respectable performance in her GCSE exams and her later success at college, some of her teachers bemoaned the fact that she had been 'held back' by the other two. Presumably, if she had not cared for her compatriots, she would already be prime minister. This last point has real significance as well as sarcasm; where people feel instinctively that something is not appropriate, they may hang on to their opinion even in the face of proof to the contrary. In schools with few bilingual pupils, beliefs such as this one may well persist and anyone wishing to make innovations needs to be forearmed with good arguments.

2. 'If bilingual pupils are placed together in language groups, they won't speak English' They certainly won't speak just English all day, that much is true. Would we want them to? Consider the results of being able to hypothesise, brainstorm or plan in your own language versus the results of attempting this in a foreign language. Consider how relaxing it is to compare notes on the latest gossip or the freshest trends with a peer or peer group when you share some common cultural references. Teachers influence English progress by organising the content of lessons to encourage the development of academic Standard English. This may involve moving pupils into different groups for different purposes, perhaps splitting up a bilingual pair at times, perhaps keeping them together at other times, in the same way that we regularly make decisions about who should work with whom during each activity.

3. *'The system places too much stress on the buddy'* This is only true of a mismanaged buddy system, where the characters involved are ill matched, or the staff are not able to support it, or the parameters have not been clarified.

Using interpreters (KS 1, 2, 3 and 4)

There is a vast difference between areas in the funding and organisation of interpreters. Some schools employ specifically trained bilingual teaching assistants with years of experience. Some schools employ teaching assistants who happen to be bilingual and can lend a hand. Some schools come to an arrangement with a local contact. Some authorities pay for temporary use of a paid interpreter to support schools. Some schools manage without.

Again, however, the organisation of such support is the most difficult part of the operation. Someone needs to plan, co-ordinate and trouble-shoot. In a secondary school, this will involve liaising with a number of different teaching and non-teaching staff in order to establish their requirements and to ensure the proper use of the interpreter. It would be a shame to invest in an interpreter (whether that cost is in time or in money) only to find that s/he had not been given the information necessary to do his/her job because one department did not understand the situation or was not ready on time. This is another example of how planning for a beginner requires the active support of management staff.

The next thing to consider is how much interpreting time is available. For the purposes of this guide, we will assume that the school has obtained a limited amount of time by approaching a bilingual adult living in the community, who will be paid as a sessional worker. This state of affairs is much more common than that of the schools who can deploy and train their own staff. Assuming, therefore, that interpreting time will be limited, it is important to avoid dependency in either the child or the teacher. There is no point in starting to depend on someone who will be gone in three weeks. For this reason, the interpreter should not visit the school every day. As a rule of thumb in Tameside, where our funding is limited, we usually recommend a total of 12 hours, spread over four to six weeks, depending on the circumstances. After 12 hours we hold a review, and if there are problems the time is extended a little.

Given the restrictions, it is important to use the time well. General in-class support sets up false expectations and results in dependency very quickly, so it is to be avoided. The best use of an interpreter is for induction. Returning to Maslow's hierarchy of needs, we can see how quickly some of those early needs of the pupil could be met by having a friendly adult there to explain in his/her preferred language. Here are some examples of real tasks performed by interpreters in real schools during the last academic year:

- Introducing the pupil to the kitchen staff and allowing him to taste some of the foods before dinnertime.

- Explaining safety rules in a laboratory.
- Explaining the system of lockers for outdoor clothing and storage.
- Giving an outline of the timetable and different subjects.
- Showing the pupil how to use the panic file.

The interpreter may also be able to provide teachers with some of the information they need to help meet the pupil's later needs of belonging and self-esteem. It is extremely important, for example, to guarantee that the interpreter will be on site ready to welcome the pupil on the first day. Here are other real tasks with the same kind of focus:

- Making labels in the preferred language (even pupils too young to read will recognise 'their' alphabet).
- Facilitating a simple board game with a group.
- Facilitating conversations between the new pupil and classmates.
- Telling the teacher more about what the pupil can do in the preferred language.
- Drawing the teacher's attention to relevant cultural information.
- Allowing the pupil to ask questions.
- Facilitating communication with the parents.
- Introducing the pupil to library or reading book arrangements.

The interpreter can also perform tasks which enable the pupil to make a good start and save the teacher some time:

- Make sure the pupil has appropriate PC skills.
- Make a bilingual glossary, or bilingual cards for a card reader.
- Give the pupil a brief introduction to the next topic.
- Give the pupil a summary of the topic just completed.
- Read dual-text stories, give rough translations of stories, or tape stories to be used later.
- Translate what the pupil has written in the preferred language.

One person, therefore, has to take responsibility for:

- identifying tasks appropriate to the situation, by liaising with other adults involved;
- discussing these with the interpreter;
- making and sharing a formal record;
- listening to feedback from the interpreter, then acting on the information;
- making sure the interpreter is given all the information and resources s/he needs;
- checking that the interpreting tasks have been successfully carried out.

In Tameside, we use a proforma to record our plans (see Fig. 5.2). This can be copied and shared by all those involved, saving precious time during the teaching day.

School	
Staff contact:	
Interpreter:	
Start date:	
Review date:	

Interpreting Tasks:

Figure 5.2   Interpreting proforma

A lot of things need to happen, therefore, in that short breathing space before Participle starts his new school. It may be that there will not be time to accomplish everything; in which case the staff at Future Perfect will prioritise using these criteria:

First priority: Anything directly affecting his daily comfort.

Second priority: Anything which will reduce stress on Participle and on his teachers.

4. Participle starts school.

In an ideal world, he will start school with a full panic file, the use of an interpreter for a couple of hours a week and two friendly chaps eager to be his buddies. All the adults in the school know he is a beginner and some of them have learned to greet him in his preferred language. Participle goes into his new class, he has his own place and he knows it. Day by day, the carefully prepared systems help him to adjust socially and to begin to access his lessons through English. Day by day, feedback about his welfare and progress comes through these same systems. The hardest part of teaching Participle was done before he arrived.

In these early weeks, his teachers understand that his learning priorities are about adjustment. They also know that many people in his position go through what is called a 'silent period', in which they listen closely but are not yet ready to speak, so they do not put undue pressure on him. They continue to speak to him, and to give him opportunities to speak without forcing him to reply. His teachers also know how exhausting school is for Participle, so they do not attempt to keep him busy for the whole session. They allow him to concentrate in small bursts, then to watch and listen, or to use his panic file. Nobody even thinks about any kind of assessment for half a term.

In the real world, Participle will start a school as near as possible to the ideal, and he will probably cope very well.

5. After the honeymoon.

After about half a term, Participle's teachers will hold a review. They will all re-mark on how quickly he has made progress and how they would hardly recognise him from the shy little thing that started all those weeks ago. Some will suspect that he secretly understood a lot of English all the time . . .

CHAPTER 6

Teaching a beginner

According to the NASSEA Steps Assessment System, beginners are said to be at Step 1. Appropriate long-term aims for pupils at Step 1 include:

- To become successfully adjusted to the new environment, making some use of the facilities on offer, interacting appropriately with a peer group and starting to be independent in some areas.

- To access the curriculum via key visuals and the pupil's preferred language/s.

(For the full list, see Chapter 4, p. 28.)

From these, we draw short-term targets, including:

- To settle into school routine.
- To take the lead from peers and respond to 'buddies'.
- To learn some frequently used nouns associated with the classroom.
- To understand English print reads from left to right and top to bottom.
- To respond to information in print.
- To find items such as the title, the writer's name, etc. from a book.
- To respond to pictures or diagrams appropriately.
- To use a library system or similar.

How and if these are to be achieved will depend on variables such as the age of the pupil and his/her existing knowledge, skills and experiences.

Which strategies teachers choose to adopt will depend on subject areas, resources and the nature of the class as a whole as well as on individual preferences and skills. The following suggestions are therefore deliberately non-specific in order that they can be read and used by teachers in any curriculum area, at any key stage. They are followed by real examples of work done with beginners in a variety of contexts.

The following points need to be kept in mind; they are the bedrock to good practice at this stage:

- This pupil already knows a great deal. Those skills and experiences can be mined in order to develop new skills and knowledge.

- Every lesson, every session, is an English Language learning opportunity, whether it is Maths, Music, a mealtime or macramé.

- Beginners can have access to at least some of the curriculum, if we engineer it.

When operating in English, the Step 1 learner will be working in the style of the 'jigsaw puzzler' (see Chapter 1, p. 4). This means tasks will involve naming, sequencing and sorting. Learning at this stage will need heavy contextual support and should therefore be visual and practical. It will not always be possible to gauge the pupil's responses to lesson content as thoroughly as many teachers would like at this stage.

Examples of lessons

The following are examples of real lessons. Many of the activities chosen will be familiar in some way. Having a beginner in the class does not mean the teacher has to redesign a whole timetable or write a new syllabus. These lessons are normal! They have some particular features in common, however. These are the features we would associate with good practice for language development in all pupils. Some elements and considerations may be less familiar to teachers with specialisms not traditionally regarded as 'language based'. These elements are much more specific to teaching EAL pupils and will be pointed out as we go along.

Key Stage 1

Adverb was a boy from Pakistan in Year 1. His teacher included him in the Literacy Hour by differentiation and by planning for language development during the following sequence of lessons. As you will see, the sequence was covered over several lessons. She chose to abandon the classic shape of the Literacy Hour during this time, but had she wished to, she could have plotted the sequence more or less into that shape, as it includes word-level, sentence-level and text-level work in all language skills. She chose the content to reflect his prior knowledge – the class made, then talked and wrote about lassi, a drink popular in many Asian-heritage families.

1   The class sat in a circle. They were shown a jug full of lassi and invited to look at it and smell it. They were asked what it was like. They were invited to drink some and comment on it. A collection of words was made. These included adjectives like 'white', 'tart', 'sweet', 'thick' and 'milky' as well as value judgements such as 'nice' and 'yucky'. There were also some qualifiers such as 'a bit' and 'really'. There was an opportunity to extend and improve vocabulary for English-speaking pupils while Adverb concentrated on more obvious items, including 'white' and 'cold'.

2   The pupils were given a small blank book made from folded paper. They made a title, drew a picture, labelled it, and then decorated it with the words they had selected to describe the lassi.

3   The class discussed what the ingredients might be and made a list to keep for later.

4   The real ingredients were brought in and named. The class compared them with their earlier guesses. Flash cards with the correct nouns were used to play games: they matched cards to ingredients; they had to cover their eyes then guess which one had been hidden; they were given a card and then asked where it belonged.

5   A big book, Jane Asher's *Round the World Cookbook* was introduced. The class used the cover, contents page, etc. in the usual way. They revised the list of ingredients. They looked at the list of utensils and played another set of games with flash cards and the real utensils.

6   The class sat in a circle again. They followed the instructions and made a big jug of lassi. This was easier than it might sound, as most children did not need to do much more than stir a bowl half full of liquid. While this was done, digital photos were taken of each stage. (NB: At the time of writing, parental permission is needed to do this.)

7   Still in the circle, the pupils revised what they had done. This involved mime and flash cards, which were used in several ways, e.g. the teacher held up the card and said 'mime this one!' At other times, she mimed an action and asked them to choose the matching flash card. The target for Adverb was to practise verbs such as 'stir', 'pour', 'beat' and 'add'. Other pupils were expected to produce longer contributions; the most complex being 'beat it well with a wooden spoon'. By the end of this section, the class had a large collection of flash cards, which could be used as prompts for simple labelling tasks or to enable the construction of longer sentences. They were colour coded according to parts of speech, then stuck to the wall.

8   The class admired large versions of some of the photos and revised what the pupils had done in each one. Here, the teacher had to choose between carrying on with the grammatical structures which were used in the recipe instructions (e.g. 'stir in the sugar', 'measure the yoghurt') or changing to the structures which would be used if giving an account of what the class had done (e.g. 'Pronoun stirred in the sugar, Article measured the yoghurt'). On this occasion, it was decided that instructions would be more supportive of Adverb's needs, so everyone was told that the photos were to help them give instructions. This kind of decision is often new to teachers who have not experienced working with EAL beginners before. In some ways, it would not have mattered which form had been chosen; the important thing was to choose one and keep to it. When teaching monolingual classes, it would not confuse the pupils if a teacher made a change, but bilingual pupils can have real difficulties when forms are inexplicably switched. It should also be pointed out that modelling and keeping to a form in this way is very supportive of the writing process for all pupils. The teacher modelled sequencing activities with the photographs, which gave a natural opportunity to revise vocabulary and sentence structures.

9   The class moved into groups. On each table there were smaller versions of the photos to sequence. Following this, the pupils were able to make up sentences for each photo. A variety of writing and reading tasks were available to use – some pupils could match sentences to photos, some could fill in blanks, some could write sentences supported by the flash cards on the wall. Adverb labelled items in the photos. Some of these he could copy from flash cards, some he could cut out and stick.

10 By the end of the sequence, the pupils had made little illustrated recipe books about lassi. The large photos were used for an interactive display. Work could then continue on other recipes.

Sequences similar to this one have been taught by teachers in different schools. Each one will be slightly different because each teacher will add his or her own style and choice of emphasis. Some will, for example, tailor the lessons to fit a traditional-style Literacy Hour. Some will include more levels of differentiation than others; some will increase the content of mime and games. Whatever changes in format are made, the principles remain the same. This kind of sequence works because:

- it is practical, concrete and visual;

- it is oracy based;

- literacy activities use language items that have been well-practised orally;

- information and language items are revisited, revised and repeated;

- the whole sequence is logical and all the work stems from something real which the pupils experienced;

- it built on something familiar to Adverb (which was not so unfamiliar to anyone else, since lassi is a kind of milkshake).

Key Stage 2

This class was studying the Egyptians. Preposition had recently arrived from Thailand with only a few words of English. The teacher had a good stock of picture books available so all the class could browse for impressions of this period of history. This sequence of lessons used peer support and differentiation to allow Preposition access to the curriculum.

1. Snowball

Each pupil had a small poster containing a little information, some with just a few words illustrated by pictures, some with rather sophisticated content for the more able. There were about ten posters altogether; most were duplicated, some more than once. Preposition had a very short one, which she could memorise quickly. The information was connected to basic ideas about Egypt which would crop up in later lessons or which some pupils might already have as part of their general knowledge, e.g. the whereabouts of Egypt, something about the Nile, about Pharaohs, gods, mummies, pyramids . . .

Each pupil had to tell as many others as possible the information on his/her poster. After about five or ten minutes, each pupil had to sit down alone and record (in writing, in picture form or in Thai, if preferred) everything they had been told. After another five minutes, the pupils were asked to share their list with a partner and see how many items they had. After five more minutes, the twos became fours and each group had nearly all the information. By now, Preposition had heard the information expressed three times (at least). She may not have understood all of it, but she had a good chance of taking in part of it, and she had been engaged in at least a short communication with a great many pupils in the class. Some of the key words were now beginning to be established. The finished rough lists of information made by the groups were displayed for a few days so that the pupils could revisit them.

This activity can be modified in various ways to suit the teacher's wishes or the nature of the class. One way to end it is to make a class list of information. When making lists on the board, it may be useful to remember that these work especially well when all the items are expressed in the same sentence structure. This models useful patterns for bilingual pupils to pick up, and supports any writing the class may be doing later. For example this list:

> They irrigated the fields
>
> They made mummies
>
> They believed in many gods

works better than:

> irrigation
>
> made mummies
>
> many gods

2. Jigsaw

This is a popular group-working activity. To prepare for this, the pupils were asked to provide as many answers as they could to the question 'What were the Egyptians famous for?' The answers were sorted into two columns, one for wealth and culture, one for climate and physical conditions. This was done quickly, as a whole-class discussion, but it could be done in two parts, first collecting the ideas, then asking groups or pairs to sort cards depicting the ideas expressed as pictures or text.

Next, the pupils were divided into mixed-ability groups of four. These were called the 'home groups'. In this class, the teacher had arranged the groups carefully to enable her to direct each pupil to an appropriately differentiated activity. Each pupil was given one of four different topics. They then had to leave their home groups, to join groups made up of other pupils working on the same topic. These were called 'expert groups'.

The four topics were:

The farmer's year

Making bricks and papyrus

Saving water

What made Egypt a rich country?

Each topic required the pupils to perform a task. The first two were the most straightforward, requiring only the transfer of information from a simple text to a chart. Preposition was in the second group, as this was the most pictorial topic. The third topic required finding information in a long text. The fourth involved piecing together information from different sources and understanding what the information inferred. All the resources the pupils needed were provided; they did not need to leave their expert group to find materials or information. These tasks were tightly focused. All the pupils in the group had to help each other to complete the task. Once the task was completed, the pupils had to prepare to take the information back to their home groups. This involved some rehearsal of how they were going to explain it. It was stressed that the expert groups would only be successful if everyone was able to complete the task and then share the information.

Next, the pupils returned to their home groups. Each home group now contained four 'experts' in different topics. They had to pool their information in order to complete a new task. This time, they were given a large poster with a representation of the river in the middle and the words 'Egypt is the gift of the Nile'. The pupils used their information to complete the poster. Preposition was able to play her part since she had been coached to say a few things in the expert group and she had her completed chart to show the group. Because she had to explain how the Egyptians had made certain things, she had to produce simple repetitive sentences in the past tense. This gave a grammatical focus to her History topic.

This group work ended here, but it could have been expanded to include a simple presentation by each group and a follow-up quiz for individual completion.

This sequence worked for the whole class, but it met Preposition's needs because:

- her work within the topic had been differentiated, without excluding her from some of the more complex ideas;
- there was a focus on some specific grammatical structures;
- ideas and language items were repeated and transferred from one medium to another;
- there were opportunities for communication with peers and peer support;
- there were plenty of pictures to help her understand the text and to prompt her to speak;
- because Preposition had specific, meaningful tasks with a language focus, there were opportunities for her teacher to observe and assess her progress in terms of language behaviour and acquisition/use of some language items.

Jigsaw group work lends itself to a variety of age groups and curriculum areas. It is just as useful with more fluent speakers of English and can be designed to suit the needs of different classes or different situations. In this example, care had been taken to differentiate the tasks given to each expert group. On another occasion, the teacher might choose to have mixed-ability expert groups. She could allow the pupils to choose their own home groups so that they become strongly motivated to supply their friends with the very best they can bring back from the expert groups. She could make the home group's task more structured or more open-ended. She could allow an element of choice in how they presented their material.

Key Stage 3

The following examples are taken from a unit of work on *A Midsummer Night's Dream*. The beginner bilingual pupil was able to join in with the class to a certain extent, and to learn some English during the lessons. She could not, in honesty, have engaged closely with the rich layers of imagery we adults enjoy in Shakespeare, but then, not a large percentage of Year 9 did.

One large wall space was devoted to a display. We started with a simple background of green and blue sugar paper, representing grass, sky and a bit of a river. Once the pupils had seen the BBC 'animated tales' version (1999, directed by Nikoli Serebrinkov) they were ready to add some specific locations, for example, the 'bank where the wild thyme blows', and some general items they thought might be found in a magic wood (mostly odd-looking trees). Discussing what the places might look like and what labels to stick on them enabled the monolingual pupils to appreciate and remember some items of the plot and some quotations. The bilingual pupil was learning much more practical English and practising some handwriting skills. We did not lay much stress on the quality of the artwork, but once we started to stick it to the background, the class grew very pleased with it. A similar process gave us a range of cutout characters, which we could stick down and label or move around to show the plot's different locations. At the same time, some of the labels were extended into captions, so that the figure of Titania had a short description of some of her characteristics. The display was starting to become a reference tool as well as a response to the story. Later, some pupils enjoyed copying out some significant quotes to stick there.

The bilingual pupil had now moved on to very simple worksheets, which some other pupils could also benefit from. She had learned to recognise 'tick the true sentence' and 'fill in the blanks'. The worksheets used these formats with repetitive sentences, starting as simply as 'Helena is a ___', with 'girl' being available in a list with the other words for blank filling. Matching, remembering and linking words to visuals are good places for beginners to start; so early worksheets depend heavily on matching- and sequencing-type exercises.

The class also tried some group work. More ideas concerning group work can be found in Chapter 7. Each group had been given a moment in the story to illustrate as a tableau. This involved reading the text closely and working together to decide how the different characters should be positioned. The bilingual pupil was not able to join in the full discussion, but benefited from being with her peers and using, if nothing else, the language of movement and position. The groups took turns to visit each other's tableaux and ask questions. Even a beginner can cope with 'Who are you?' 'I am Hermia' or 'How are you feeling?' 'I love Lysander'. To develop this further, and to re-use some of the expressions practised in making the tableaux, the groups were asked to position themselves into plot order. They had their photos taken in their roles, and the pictures were used to generate written work at various levels.

Useful advice about Shakespeare and bilingual learners can be found in *Bilingual Shakespeare* (Fellowes 2001).

Additional adults

It might be tempting to use additional adults simply to help the pupil get through the lesson. Once called in some circles the 'whispering radiator' model, this certainly has some advantages. It lightens the teacher's workload, reduces stress and makes beginners at least look as if they are well integrated. Yes, it might even be appropriate under some conditions, but, as they say, is it art? There is quite a lot wrong with this style of support as a long-term strategy, and there is plenty right with dozens of more considered approaches.

Let us first consider who these additional adults might be. Leaving out those working under an SEN arrangement, not involved with bilingual pupils unless they have special needs, the list could include:

- Teaching assistants.
- Teaching assistants who happen to be bilingual.
- Bilingual teaching assistants who specialise in working with bilingual pupils.
- Parents.
- Volunteers.
- Interpreters.
- Teachers.
- EAL teachers.
- Learning mentors.

It is a fairly obvious point at its most basic level: we can expect different kinds of support from different adults we work with. It will be no surprise to anyone to be told that a parent helper will undertake different tasks from a qualified, experienced TA. Looking at the differences between what a TA (bilingual) and a specialist Bilingual Assistant will be able to do may be uncharted ground, however. Making assumptions about the roles of other adults can lead to giving them too much responsibility, or too little opportunity. For example, consigning an EAL teacher to a whispering radiator model of support is a waste of their skills, not to mention a waste of taxpayers' money.

If you have an opportunity to work with another adult, for however long or short the involvement, you will find that s/he comes with particular expectations about what kinds of intervention are expected or are appropriate. Consider these stories:

Teacher number one was given two hours a week TA help for his bilingual pupil at Step 3 for all English skills. He began by sharing a working lunch with the TA. They discussed their previous experiences of working with bilingual pupils, and found that they were both inexperienced. The TA was given an opportunity to say what her strengths were, however, and to make sure the teacher understood her working conditions and arrangements. Using this information, the teacher was able to pick a parcel of strategies and activities which suited all concerned. The TA spent half an hour each week with the pupil revising vocabulary learned in other lessons in order to build English reading skills, and another half an hour revising or preparing for topics to be covered, making good use of key visuals. The other hour was spent in class, facilitating collaborative group work. The arrangements were reviewed regularly.

Teacher number two was given two hours a week TA help for his bilingual pupil at Step 3 for all English skills. He began by introducing her to the class and making space for her to sit near the pupil. He treated her with consideration and respect, but she spent the next term as a whispering radiator as she and the teacher clumsily tried to approach each other through a fog of mistaken roles and wrong assumptions. After this long period of adjustment, she was able to work out some useful strategies to support the pupil.

People resources are the most precious, and often the scarcest. Spend time at the beginning in order to gain the most from each minute later. Lists of teaching strategies for each step can be found in Chapter 4, but here is a list of things additional adults could do, depending on variables such as experience, qualifications and terms of employment:

- Deliver the lesson, leaving you free to work with the bilingual pupil, or to assess EAL progress.
- Help you to prepare lessons with language content in mind.
- Focus on one group during collaborative work.
- Prepare materials for collaborative work.
- Help with classroom organisation during collaborative work.
- 'Prime the pump', i.e. use visual resources to set the scene for new topics to be covered or introduce vocabulary for new topics.
- Revise vocabulary used during the last few days, using it as a source for literacy work.
- Prepare and help the pupil to maintain individual word lists and dictionaries.
- Give individual support for homework.
- Supervise use of card readers or bilingual tapes.
- Read dual-text books, and then use the story or pictures as a source for literacy work.
- Work closely with the bilingual pupil, ensuring s/he has access to the highest level of work.
- Model speech for the pupil.
- Prompt the pupil to speak in connected utterances.
- Supervise shared writing.
- Supervise paired reading.
- Make cards for card readers.
- Facilitate use of interactive displays.
- Facilitate use of appropriate computer programs.
- Review written work with the pupil, extending the range of syntax.

This list is not exhaustive. With opportunities like these, it is easy to see why the focused use of additional adults is so much more efficient as well as preferable in terms of interest and enrichment for all concerned. It is worth noting here that, depending on when they were trained, some TAs may well have been given more time to explore child development and its implications for learning than some teachers. Potentially, this gives such teachers an ideal opportunity to broaden their own horizons.

Auditing resources

Some thought needs to be given to the choice of resources. Although few of us have the luxury of being able to purchase exactly the right resource exactly when we discover we need it, there are general principles to bear in mind which are fairly obvious if you put yourself in the pupil's shoes:

1   Clarity: Imagine learning to read with a new alphabet. You have just built up a little confidence, then suddenly you are asked to read letters with curly bits and wobbly bits on unnecessarily fussy, crowded pages. One curly bit will be of interest; you will learn a little about style for later on when you become fluent. Too much will be confusing.

2   Visuals: These are of vital importance. If you cannot understand when someone tells you about a hanging valley, then looking at a picture of it will help you to learn, not just about the hanging valley, but about all the words that person uses to describe it, such as steep, flat, waterfall, etc. Similarly, a graph, table, chart or diagram will not just explain a thousand words; it will prompt a thousand words, if used well. The more realistic pictures are the better. The less assumptions made the better. The more there is to talk about the better.

3   Content: Make it as appropriate as possible. Learning through an additional language does not imply slow development of any kind. It may imply some differences of culture, which is why factual books related to the pupil's own experiences at home or at school are usually better than, for example, fantasy fiction. What is good for bilingual pupils is usually good for everyone else as well, but not always vice-versa.

4   Repetition: A huge help. If you can predict what the words are going to be, you will be able to understand and perhaps read more. We all know this about traditional tales, but it is also true about some Science texts, recipes, songs, poems and text in other genres. Repetitive formats are safe as well as supportive, giving confidence along with plenty of clues.

5   Bias: Important for all learners as well as their educators, resources should be vetted for bias of all varieties before purchase. Nobody will get very far if they are subtly being told there is something a bit peculiar about them. This is not an appropriate topic to cover in depth in a book focused on language issues, but excellent advice can be gathered from several sources, including publications from Trentham Books and the Development Education Project in Manchester (see Useful Contacts, p. 102).

Beginners at Key Stage 4

Pupils new to English arriving in Year 10 or 11 tend to be either the most worried-about pupils in the country or completely ignored. Neither attitude is very helpful, but they do need some special consideration.

First, check that all the information you have is accurate. It is surprisingly rare for a pupil to arrive at this age with absolutely no English. You may have a pupil with very limited English, or one who is illiterate in English, or one who can only cope with English in written forms. Make sure you know what the pupil's skills are, and remember that they may take time to adjust to the varieties of spoken English in your school.

Assuming the pupil is a true beginner, a decision has to be made about what they want from their time during KS 4. They may already have clear opinions about this. Do they want to use the time to gather enough English and cultural knowledge to enable them to succeed at GCSE a little later? Do they want to push themselves enough to achieve some GCSEs now? Do they see this time as preparation, or as their only education in the UK? The wishes of the pupil or the family will inform the school's arrangements. The flexibility of the curriculum in different institutions is also an important variable; this changes over time and is in turn affected by factors such as how many bilingual pupils a school has. A school with many bilingual pupils, whether beginners or not, would be expected to have systems and resources supportive of late arrivals. A school with little or no experience of this may not have the same range of opportunities. All the following arrangements have been made in some schools. Some may be suitable or possible in yours:

- Pupils concentrated on a limited GCSE programme with the idea that even a low grade would indicate their commitment and rate of progress.
- Pupils attended ESOL courses at a nearby college for part of the week.
- Pupils took a GCSE in their own language.
- Pupils studied a commercial EFL course on tape instead of some lessons.
- Pupils attended practical courses at a nearby college for most of the week.
- Pupils took the usual timetable, with support directed to subjects considered to be most important to them.
- Pupils concentrated on practical courses, using them as a focus for acquiring English.
- Pupils moved to Year 9 instead of joining in Year 10, in order to gain some English before starting KS 4.
- Pupils attended Year 10 twice.

Some of these choices will be inappropriate, being unsuitable to the pupil's wishes or unworkable given the current systems operating in different schools. Some would be considered unsound in certain circumstances. What they do show, however, is that there are different models we can adopt to address the wishes of late arrivals.

SUMMARY

To conclude this chapter on the education of beginners, we would like to emphasise one key element of EAL: *understanding, activating and building on a pupil's existing knowledge and skills is the foundation of good practice.*

CHAPTER 7

Ways of moving on

Pupils stuck in the middle: Step 4

'The teachers don't understand. They think I can do all the work.'

These words were spoken by Calligraphy, a French-speaking Year 8 pupil during her second term in an English school. Her previous education had been in French. Her second language was Flemish and she had a working knowledge of Arabic. On arrival in school in this country, she was assessed within NASSEA Step 2. With support, she made excellent progress. Within two terms, she was working towards Step 5. By the end of this second term, teaching staff deemed her to be 'fine'.

Information acquired on admission established she had attended a French-medium school abroad from the age of six. She was used to school routines. She had well-established literacy and oracy skills in her first language. She had made good progress. She had good social skills and this, together with her confidence and strong family support, enabled her to settle very quickly into a new school environment and make rapid progress in acquiring conversational English.

The once quiet pupil blossomed into a fairly confident one who was increasingly joining in conversations and activities with her friends. Teachers were delighted with her progress. The initial concerns of having an EAL pupil in class were quickly dismissed. However, as Calligraphy has already told us, they did not see the full picture. Calligraphy felt she was experiencing difficulties with her class work, especially with written tasks.

We have two different perspectives here, namely those of the class teacher and those of the pupil. The class teacher observed a pupil who was interacting successfully with friends at a conversational level, could give correct answers in class discussions, was gaining confidence orally and was eager to learn and achieve. All appeared well. Yet the pupil had a different perspective. While she was apparently gaining confidence in social language use, she was becoming more frustrated with the language demands of the curriculum, being unable to express her opinion fully in a second language, especially at the pace of lesson delivery at Key Stage 3. In other words, while she was able to begin to contribute to a class discussion and to grasp some elements of a lesson, she was nevertheless experiencing difficulty with the written demands of new text, new vocabulary and the linguistic and structural demands of free writing tasks.

The following example seeks to clarify how she was responding to the situation.

The class had been set a task of writing a report about their school. Calligraphy responded by writing a description about the school using all the words she could find. This was actually done to the best of her ability, although it was not exactly what had been requested. Her teacher believed she had not understood the nature of the request. The pupil, on the other hand, hoped that the teacher would be aware that the demands of the task were beyond her, so she responded by writing her own text, differentiating the task to her own level. Had she been asked to do this work in her first language, she would have been able to complete the task at a very competent level. As a pupil at Step 4, however, she was only able to produce some 'writing about school', not a considered, crafted document covering several aspects of school life and organisation.

Working towards Step 5, she could understand most conversations in class and was beginning to engage in class conversations about the curriculum to a greater extent. Both her vocabulary and sentence structures were now developing. Once the vocabulary was explained to her, she was quick to understand the underlying concept.

The following example is taken from Science. The task was to record what had happened during a practical lesson. The pupils were to establish if carbon dioxide was present in limewater. If carbon dioxide were present, then the water would turn cloudy. Understanding the concept was no problem for Calligraphy, as can be seen by her comment as she looked at her limewater: 'It got bubbles. It fog.' Her verbal answer, however short, was a confident one, instantaneous, graphic and self-explanatory. She got the message over without paying much attention to grammatical English. It was a good start, but her written description of the practical, without any intervention or support, might also have been 'It got bubbles. It fog.'

Calligraphy was confident in conversation, especially when the subject was very obvious. Would she be sufficiently confident and knowledgeable in order to write up her Science practical? The chances are she would find this level of work rather challenging. The language demands of describing a scene, a character, an experiment, or summarising a story content would involve a much greater knowledge of English vocabulary and syntax than she currently possesses. These tasks use higher-order language skills which Calligraphy may already have in her own language. However, her English will not be fluent enough for her to utilise these skills without scaffolding provision to support thinking. This is typical of the pupil between Steps 4 and 5. They are literally stuck in the middle, between the early survival skills and the sophisticated manipulation of facts, opinions and ideas they will undertake as they develop true fluency. The huge step forward this represents takes much longer than those early advances, when the pupil appeared to stride from strength to strength.

As they move closer to Step 5, pupils develop an enriched vocabulary both in common words and subject-specific or technical words. They sustain short conversations and can produce a piece of written text unaided. However, at this stage, the quality of a piece of work carried out independently contrasts markedly with what the pupil can achieve with 'scaffolding' support. This is what Vygotsky terms the Zone of Proximal Development (ZDP) (see p. viii).

In growing closer to Step 5, Calligraphy had already advanced a long way since her arrival. To what could we attribute her success?

She was by nature a confident pupil who was not afraid to join in, who made friends very quickly, and tried out new language items. She was not afraid to make mistakes. Her starting point was actually talking initially to another child, then she spoke to others, eventually interacting with her teachers.

In other words, oracy was the key for her as a Step 2 pupil. It retains its importance beyond this early stage, however. If our pupil is to truly succeed in the system, she will need oracy skills at an academic level, which, in turn, will equip her to hypothesise, describe, evaluate, plan, compare and record. In order for her to reach her full potential we would need to ensure that oracy is an integral part of her learning process, as it is one of the major ways in which pupils make sense of their environment; it also underpins literacy development. Classroom planning is necessary to provide opportunities for interaction. Planning for oracy is one of the key practices which Calligraphy's teachers can use to help her make that huge jump between Steps 4 and 5.

Calligraphy will also need to achieve at a faster rate than her monolingual peers. They have already acquired English and are making progress year by year. For bilingual pupils, the progress curve is a rather different one. Not only do bilingual pupils need to acquire English as fast as possible, but they also have to catch up to their peers by progressing at a greater speed. No sooner have they reached one level, than they are already embarking on the next. This rate of progress, however accelerated, must always be maintained by all EAL pupils. This is what is often referred to as the 'moving target'. Bilingual learners have to work harder to bridge that ever-increasing gap if they are to succeed on a par with their monolingual peers.

Bilingual pupils do not acquire a second language by sitting quietly at the back of a classroom, or even by being taken out of the classroom and given an alternative programme. Instead they acquire English language through interaction with their peers and their learning environment. For many bilingual pupils, their only access to English is in school.

The importance of oracy

'Language is the main vehicle by which we know about other people's thoughts, and the two must be intimately related' (Pinker forthcoming).

Normally, all humans develop the capacity to talk. This is the way we exchange ideas and thoughts. It is a complex task that children begin from an early age. A safe and rich language environment in which the child can access good language role models and feel secure enough to try out new language forms is the ideal. Children rapidly become proficient at listening to new vocabulary and chunks of language and trying these out. Most bilingual pupils have already acquired their first language in exactly the same way. Depending on the pupil's age and length of education abroad, their first language can be an invaluable resource on which to build new language skills. The fact that Calligraphy had arrived with well-established skills in her first language meant she had transferable language concepts on which to build.

While there are many similarities between children learning their first and second language, there are also significant differences. Bilingual pupils have already experienced learning a first language and are effective communicators in this. However, learning an additional language usually takes place in a busy classroom where the pupil is one of a large group. Rarely will s/he have the benefit of one-to-one attention from an adult. This is why fluent peer role models and collaborative group work are so important. In addition, bilingual pupils are cognitively and conceptually on a par with their English-speaking peers. Limited English should not lead to underestimated academic expectations. Nor can limited English speech be seen as an indication of low ability, as any activity carried out in the pupil's preferred language would quickly prove.

'Language is an integral part of most learning and oral language in particular has a key role in classroom teaching and learning' (Primary National Strategy 2003). Oracy, therefore, is not only the key to the development of literacy skills; it is essential to a meaningful learning experience.

All pupils will need to become confident speakers with the ability to respond to and engage in a range of interactive situations, starting with something as simple as asking for a new pencil and leading to more demanding tasks, such as having to offer a summary of Anne Frank's diary. All pupils need to acquire good communication skills. An effective communicator has developed skills of listening comprehension and speech in both social and academic contexts.

On arrival, Calligraphy was busy acquiring basic vocabulary and phrases to allow her to make friends, and to make sense of her new learning environment. She had to be an active listener, carefully observing her peers and picking out the relevant words and phrases she would use to make herself understood. At the stage Calligraphy was reaching, establishing use of higher-order oracy skills in English was still a priority for her.

Conversational language is very different from written language. Chance conversations are informal and about topics of immediate interest to the people concerned. Conversations are not always just between two people, in fact, several people can be active participants. People usually face each other and are normally within hearing distance. Information is readily shared and sentences can be half finished. Others volunteer and finish sentences. Facial expressions and gesture play an important part in adding to any message. Intonation is particularly useful when conveying a message, especially if the person is angry or upset.

All pupils learn through being actively involved in tasks alongside their peers. They gather information by observing, listening to others and practising new vocabulary and sentence structures. It is through engaging in the interactive process of listening and speaking that children gather new information, formulate ideas, solve problems, speculate, make decisions, organise their thoughts and ideas and reflect on what is important. Active learning and oracy have an additional importance for bilingual learners.

Moving on from Step 4

Limited English does not stop EAL pupils from actively engaging in the learning process. They too can join in challenging tasks. However, at this time, the pupil may be mentally translating between two or more languages, which is in itself a cognitive challenge. If production is to be in English, some thought needs to be given to how this might be supported. Broadly speaking, the message for teachers here is to be aware of the subtle balance between having challenging language content and challenging curricular content. In order to avoid overload, teachers will sometimes have to choose which elements to emphasise.

We need to recognise the duality of EAL learning. Bilingual pupils are learning English, which for them is an additional language. At the same time, they are using this additional language to learn the same curriculum as everyone else.

Let us examine a transcript of a Year 3 Thai-speaking pupil who is in the process of mastering conversational English and moving towards academic English. He is assessed at NASSEA Step 4. The following piece of work was transcribed following considerable individual scaffolding support throughout one term. The story of Goldilocks and the Three Bears had been studied by a group of children. The vocabulary and new sentence structures had been introduced and the children had had considerable practice in sequencing the pictures and re-telling the story. The set of six pictures taken from *Responding to Traditional Tales, Key Stage One* (O'Toole and Coote 1994) was used in this instance. The following is an example of the child's speech, as he retold the story, unaided, in his own words.

Goldilocks and the Three Bears

Bears go to walk . . . in some park or somewhere . . . and the girl's come in and clock the door and she try big one, it's too cold, she's a so hot, and she try small one, and she's just right and she eat all of it – finished!

She sit on the big chair and she – it's too hard and the – it's for middle one and it's too soft, and she sit on small chair and the break.

She sleep on the big one, it's too big and she sleep on the middle one, it's too soft, and she sleep on the small bed and she sleep on it and when Teddy said then want to go home . . .

Then see no and she's the, Daddy Bear said 'someone eat my porridge' and Mummy Bear said 'someone eat my porridge', Baby Bear said 'someone eat all of my porridge – all gone.'

Then go upstairs . . . and she . . . 'someone sit on my chair' and Mummy Bear 'someone sit on my chair'.

Baby Bear said 'and here's chair. So broke.' And then go upstairs. She's run away to she's house!

This delightful story gives us a picture of the child's oral English. It would be unrealistic to expect this child to be able to re-tell the story without first having the story introduced, and then the vocabulary and sentence structures isolated and practised.

How do we help this pupil to move on to the next step?

In order to improve his present version of Goldilocks and the Three Bears, the following could happen:

- He could listen to the story and pick out details of comparisons and descriptions (e.g. hard, softer, smaller, etc.). The adult reading the story would leave oral blanks for the group of children to fill in in chorus.

- He could complete a version of the story or a similar story, using common connectives, e.g. 'And', 'but', 'so', 'next', 'then', 'first', etc.

- He could be coached in using verb tenses correctly, following modelling by peers or adults.

- He could use figurines or puppets and re-tell the main sequences in a group.

- He could join in a paired reading session using this story.

- He could go through a series of activities involving matching, sequencing, reading, writing and re-forming using pictures and text. This can be done with a grammatical emphasis or with a factual emphasis.

- He could engage in shared writing.

In order to facilitate these activities, the story would be presented with good quality pictures. These activities would teach, practise and consolidate vocabulary, sentence structure, pronunciation and intonation for all the pupils in the class.

Extending speech

Let us give some thought to what we actually do when young children are in the early stages of acquiring their first language. We help them by giving them support as and when they require it, mainly by providing good language models, providing alternative vocabulary and, even more importantly, extending their language. We then give them the opportunity to use that new language and praise them for their efforts. We can take the example of a very young child asking for a drink:

Child:	Drink.
Parent:	Do you want a drink? Do you want some orange juice, milk or some water?
Child:	Drink, juice.
Parent:	Would you like a drink of orange juice? Would you like your juice in a cup?
Child:	Juice in cup.
Parent:	Here you are, orange juice in a cup.
	(Child takes drink)
Parent:	Where's the magic word?
Child:	Thank you.

The child began by saying one word, 'Drink'. This is what he could say unaided. However, the adult offering a whole choice of words and then asking the same question again, helps the child not only to acquire new vocabulary and new sentence structures but also to try out this language for himself. The adult had to be prepared to be patient and offer alternatives. While the child could say one word unaided, with support he is able to use extended language. It is an example of the difference between what a learner can do alone and what he can do with support. This is a very effective technique which can be used with all children at every level, and even more so with bilingual learners.

This model can be modified for older pupils in far more demanding situations. Let us return to Calligraphy with her science experiment and examine how her single answer could have been developed.

Pupil:	It got bubbles. It fog.
Teacher:	That's right. I can see bubbles too. I can also see that the limewater has turned cloudy. What happened to the limewater?
Pupil:	It turned cloudy.
Teacher:	What actually turned cloudy? Do you mean the limewater turned cloudy?
Pupil:	The limewater turned cloudy.
Teacher:	Can you remember what it means when the limewater turns cloudy? Does it mean there is carbon dioxide?
Pupil:	Yes.
Teacher:	Yes there is . . .
Pupil:	Carbon dioxide.
Teacher:	Tell me in a sentence.
Pupil:	There is carbon dioxide.
Teacher:	Have I got this right? The limewater turned cloudy because there is carbon dioxide in it.
Pupil:	Yes.
Teacher:	Now you tell me about it.
Pupil:	The limewater turned cloudy. There is carbon dioxide.
Teacher:	Can you use 'because' in your sentence?
Pupil:	The limewater turned cloudy because there is carbon dioxide.
Teacher:	Well done.

By offering subject-specific vocabulary and sentence structure, and maintaining the conversation to several turns, we can extend the pupil's English language using this simple but effective technique.

Extending writing

Similarly, in order to help Calligraphy to improve her literacy skills, the following activities might be considered:

- She could listen to a class presentation and respond appropriately to questions or fill in a sheet showing she had understood.
- She could isolate new vocabulary, use a dual-language dictionary and maintain a word list.
- She could use a writing frame.

- She could sequence key words to create her own writing frame. This could have a grammatical basis, e.g. using common connectives like 'first' and 'then', or using verb tenses, like 'mixed' or 'heated'.

- She could read a passage, marking the key vocabulary or structures.

- She could re-tell the experiment to another pupil in preparation to writing it down.

- She could explain how she would be tackling the task before she did it, using an adult or peer model.

- She could tape her commentary and follow up with one or more of the following: scribing, transcript, word processing, oral correction.

These activities are concerned with isolating and practising vocabulary or structures, about rehearsing writing and about scaffolding English production. They are likely to benefit all pupils in the class as well as Calligraphy. They form a crucial link between oracy and literacy.

Science is a fruitful area for language development as practical lessons precede abstract conclusions, or generalisations. As we have seen, Calligraphy was able to make an observation of the limewater, and then draw a conclusion. She learned language as well as Science by doing this. Key visuals are not just pictures but any concrete resources that support meaning. The term therefore includes practical activities and demonstrations as well as charts, tables and pictures. All these help pupils move from the concrete to the abstract. Language is an abstract system. To develop new language items, the learner first visits the concept at a concrete level.

Additional suggestions for moving pupils on at Step 4

There are a number of simple rules that are really useful:

- Treat the pupil like the others in the class. Even if s/he does not speak fluently in English, s/he is likely to understand, if supported.

- Please do not ignore the pupil. There is nothing worse than ignoring a child either in a lesson or in school.

- When speaking, face the pupil and speak clearly, giving time for him/her to process the language.

- Remember to engage with the pupil. Don't expect him/her to approach you; you may have to take the lead and initiate a conversation.

- Placing a bilingual pupil in a group situation significantly improves his/her chances of interacting with peers and extending language skills in a non-threatening way.

- Peer tutoring in English is invaluable if a pupil has not grasped key information. Another pupil can not only give support through revising work introduced in previous lessons, but this exercise will actually help the pupil to consolidate his/her own knowledge.

- Peer tutoring using a pupil's first language is also helpful. Older settled bilingual pupils could become an invaluable source of support for newly arrived pupils.

There is a wealth of guidance in the Primary National Strategy publication, *Speaking, Listening, Learning: working with children in Key Stages 1 and 2* (Primary National Strategy 2003). This focuses on the importance of oracy. The materials reflect the National Curriculum requirements in English and develop approaches to teaching, extending and reinforcing listening and speaking both in English and across the curriculum. In terms of teaching pupils with EAL, best use may be had from these materials by focusing on ideas which will help to develop cognitive links and language in a range of curricular contexts. In other words, language across the curriculum.

The materials include:

- a set of objectives for listening and speaking in Years 1–6;
- examples of teaching sequences for the objectives;
- a video illustrating the teaching of listening and speaking linked to some of the sequences;
- a handbook with advice on the principles behind the materials and on assessment, together with commentaries on the video;
- leaflets on four aspects of listening and speaking.

The materials are all related to the four aspects of listening and speaking in the National Curriculum programmes of study for English:

- Listening: developing active listening strategies and critical skills of analysis.
- Speaking: being able to speak clearly and to develop and sustain ideas in conversation.
- Group discussion and interaction: taking different roles in groups, making a range of contributions and working collaboratively.
- Drama: improvising and working in role, scripting and performing, and responding to performances.

Copies of these materials can be acquired through telephoning 0845 602 2260; the reference number is DfES 0626–2003 G.

Group work

Group work is strongly recommended in terms of both language development and access to the curriculum. Within a small group, learners feel less threatened and will be far more confident. Language learning takes place where language is being used for a specific purpose, rather than being studied out of context. Group work can be carefully organised so that all group members have a role to play and are expected to participate, e.g. seeker of information, reporter, recorder, timekeeper, questioner.

At the most basic level, group work can be just two or more friends helping each other. At its most complex, group work can involve long, highly sophisticated simulations, using two or three classrooms, a whole year group and several adult facilitators. In terms of teaching pupils with EAL, group work usually means collaborative group work, because this offers language development and contextual support opportunities. The Collaborative Education Project (see Useful Contacts, p. 102) is a good source of information and advice about this.

Preparation

Pupils who may have been accustomed to very formal classrooms or the simpler 'working together' styles of group work may struggle with the demands of structured groups. It is worthwhile, then, first establishing what behaviour will be expected from them and what they should be aiming for. The nature of the preparation will naturally depend on the class, subject and teacher, but the following items have all been significant in different situations at different times:

- Holding a discussion on what makes a good talker and a good listener. This will give you an opportunity to influence communicative behaviour.

- Supplying a list of what successful groups will have done, including how they will have listened to each other and shared responsibilities.

- Firmly stating that the task is not completed until all group members are confident with the material, or that every group member must complete the task.

- Having a clear list of roles and responsibilities (including tidying up!).

- Providing equipment and reference materials ready for each group, to save time and cut down on movement.

- Holding a mini-project, then giving the groups feedback, not on the completed project, but on their collaboration skills. Self-assessment can be powerful here.

- Being absolutely clear, and absolutely immoveable, about time limits.

- Raising issues about how we can make each other feel safe enough to express opinions or ideas, however tentative or unformed, so that they can be built on.

Techniques

There is a whole raft of books available on group work and oracy. One to look out for in particular is *An Introduction to Oracy*, edited by Jackie Holderness and Barbara Lalljee. Here, we will list some of the most popular techniques.

Snowball

There is an example of a snowball-like activity in Chapter 6. Like a snowball, talk is supposed to grow when it is rolled around, so in this activity, pupils share information, first with one partner, then with another pair, then with a larger group, and so on. This can be done with facts provided by the teacher, facts gleaned from a source, or ideas generated by individuals, depending on the teacher's purpose. It can be quite sedentary, with pupils turning to each other and then turning around in their chairs, or it can be completely free range, with pupils walking around. A snowball is about repetition, building confidence, practising and sharing.

Listening triads

Three pupils sit together. Pupil A has a story to tell, information to share or an opinion to explain. Pupil B has to listen, prompt, ask for clarification or details, and generally work with pupil A to make sure the fullest version of the story is given. Pupil C is not allowed to speak during this time, but has to prepare a summary of everything that was said for later. This can be written or spoken, depending on the teacher's intentions. Triads are a good way of getting information across, or of encouraging story telling. Incidentally, this strategy gives the teacher an opportunity to restrain very dominant talkers for a while. If used well and frequently, giving pupils opportunities to experience each role, triads can help pupils understand more about how listening is an activity, not a passive state.

Jigsaw

A full example of this can be found in Chapter 6. Put briefly, pupils start in one group, and then are directed to another group in which they perform a task or find information. They return to the first group, where the results from each pupil are pooled to complete a larger task. The end product can involve a production or performance if this is appropriate. It can also be rounded off with some kind of individual work. Many variations of jigsawing exist; the technique lends itself well to both fact crunching and creativity across all age ranges. It is one of the most popular kinds of group work because it enables pupils to explore meaning together and then to express the content again and again through different media, supporting both subject knowledge and language development.

Envoy

Again, this can take a variety of forms. A working group is allowed to send one member off to look for information. This could be from a library, from a PC, from an adult or even from another group. It works very well where groups have been asked to design or invent something. One version, called 'industrial spy', involves sending a representative to copy ideas! If it is organised so as to prevent resentment, it is a good way of raising achievement. Pupils acting as envoys will be exercising important skills of summarising and then verbalising what they have seen or found: this could be particularly beneficial for those EAL pupils at Step 5 and beyond.

Rainbow

This is a good way of making sure the pupils work with everyone in the class, not just their friends. It may, therefore, be a good way to introduce structured group work. Each pupil has a colour. The teacher asks colours to work together in different combinations to perform different tasks. Part of the activity will therefore involve finding the right colour groups.

This list is by no means exhaustive. The following activity has been popular in several schools, but it does not take its form from any of the above:

Points of view on the Vikings

The class is divided into four groups. Each group has a good view of one side of a box or display. The sides contain information in text, captions and pictures. They are:

Side 1: The Vikings were farmers. This is about the farming year, different tasks on the farm and tools used.

Side 2: The Vikings were travellers. This is about their boats, how they navigated, the reasons they travelled and the places they visited.

Side 3: The Vikings were cultured. This is about crafts, beliefs, artefacts, language, stories, etc.

Side 4: The Vikings were invaders. This is about the gory bits.

Each group is allowed to spend time examining and learning their side. Next, they have to elect a speaker whom they will coach to make a speech and answer questions on their topic.

The groups are then called together. Each pupil is given a sheet like this one:

Figure 7.1 The truth about the Vikings

The four speakers take their places in front of the class. The teacher takes on the role of a TV presenter, introducing them as visiting professors who are going to tell us the truth about the Vikings. Each professor makes a speech and time is given for any questions. During the speeches, the class make notes on their sheets.

A discussion follows about which professor, if any, was telling the truth. This is an opportunity to bring out a lot of important ideas about bias, about evidence and about incomplete information in History.

The sequence ends with each pupil completing a quiz based on some of the facts from each side. The four professors help individuals who are stuck.

The Points of View box could be used with opinions (for example, about whether or not wind power is a good idea), comparisons (for example, on the uses, advantages and disadvantages of four kinds of fuel) or, as in this case, to explore different facets of one topic.

SUMMARY

To conclude this chapter, we should like to emphasise the importance of *oracy* at all stages of development, for both bilingual and monolingual pupils. Oracy is a key element of EAL.

Developing CALP (Cognitive Academic Language Proficiency)

Heed this dire warning from old hands who have sailed many an EAL ocean and lived to tell the tale. Far, far away, beyond the rocky coasts where beginners rise up to shock the unwary, beyond the eerie stillness of the Step 4 to 5 doldrums, a devilish trap has sunk many a poor pupil. Fooled by calm bright water after all their perils, their reckless teachers see the way clear ahead and say to their sorry selves, 'Seems OK! Full steam ahead, me hearties!' The hapless pupil is pushed on without a lifeboat, straight into the dreaded SEEMS OK trap, only to founder and sink, bound, shipmates, to underachieve for ever.

Now we have stretched our metaphoricals, let us take a cool look at the SEEMS OK trap so we will be able to recognise it.

The SEEMS OK trap occurs in a busy classroom containing enough work for several teachers: the full range of abilities, some pupils with emotional/behavioural problems, some special needs in evidence, a few technical problems with ICT equipment, a bit of a Pritt Stick shortage, a nasty draught and an uneasy relationship with the caretaker. In this classroom is a bilingual learner. This pupil has probably been in the school for some time. His present teacher may have worked in a different school when he first arrived a few years ago. She has some records and some anecdotal evidence about his development, showing that he has made good progress. When he enters her class, he seems happy. He follows instructions without needing any help. He volunteers to answer questions. Sometimes he makes suggestions. He does his homework. He tries to be neat and tidy. He is mostly well behaved. Compared to some of the other pupils, he is delightful. He scores higher in some tests than some of his classmates. He rarely asks the teacher for help.

That is what the trap generally looks like. If, a few weeks into the term, when the teacher reviews in her head how her class is looking, she thinks of this pupil and says to herself 'Hmm, seems OK' then the trap springs shut on both of them. The teacher is no longer able to perceive the pupil's needs and the pupil will not receive the support he requires. He will be receiving the same language input as the other members of the class, who have been using English since birth. Since he has only been using English for a few years, and the school is the main (or only) place where he does use it, this input will not be adequate. Although there is some disagreement about how long it takes a pupil to acquire Cognitive Academic Language Proficiency (Cummins 1996) the most conservative estimate suggests at least seven years. Some sources claim it takes much longer. The pupil will certainly have some language needs throughout his school career. If he does not receive tuition sensitive to these needs, he will not acquire CALP fully enough to express himself or to understand the complexities of expression he will meet, especially in texts, as he moves up the system.

If he is bright and hard working, he may achieve respectable enough grades when sitting external tests. When he makes his subject choices as he gets older, he may shy away from anything he sees as wordy, even if this is where his interests lie. As a young adult, his career choices may be limited more by complex language issues than by his interests or abilities.

That is not the picture we really want for our pupils.

If he is bright and of a different mindset, he may harbour all kinds of resentments about the lack of support, which will show in his relationships with staff and pupils, especially as he grows older. We do not want that picture, either.

If he is bright and less confident, he may become withdrawn in some way. He may avoid independent communication, for fear of being shown up. He may gain a reputation for laziness or poor motivation. It may be hard to establish what he could be capable of achieving. Another bleak picture.

The SEEMS OK trap is a nasty little trick appearances play on the unwary. Forewarned against the trap, what should we look for to keep our pupils' language needs clearly visible and in the open?

Let us now examine what a classroom experience might be like. Imagine you are a pupil and you have been given the following document to read; working independently, you are to answer a whole pile of hard questions on it afterwards. As you read, make a mental note of everything that seems unusual, difficult or just plain impenetrable to you. When you have finished, scribble down what you think it was all about.

Tales from a misspent middle age

Some of my friends used to envy my spending Sunday with a bunch of beefy young men, but it had its drawbacks.

An example of this is the time we did Little Hull.

It was a walk-in, I remember, which made a pleasant change from some of the dangerous sinks they had dragged me down. There was a short pitch near the entrance. I always used a petzl stop. I don't like a figure of eight, and a rack goes too fast.

A delay followed, while something was being rigged ahead. Stuck back in the queue, I could not see. People started moving on after a while. When my turn came, I stepped up to the rigging. It was only a one-wall traverse. I showed remarkable self-restraint.

'You didn't tell me that was there,' I said, politely.

'You would not have come if we had told you,' Mick replied, logically.

My choice was a simple one: press on, or get hypothermia waiting for the driver to come up from the sump. With a sinking stomach, I unravelled my cows' tails and clicked my crabs on to the rope. The traverse was about six or eight feet across, so there were a few belays. I inched across, tiring my arm muscles by hanging on too tightly. One of my cows' tails was too short, which made it even harder.

Mick had the patience of a cross-stitcher. He talked me through every movement. I depended on him completely. I was embarrassed and terrified. I was also jealous of the ease with which Stephen was completing the traverse, just behind me. When, in a state of shock and exhaustion, I collapsed on the safe ground beyond, Stephen said, 'You know, you really impressed me.'

This was a novel idea. 'Why on earth was that?' I asked.

'Because I've never heard a lady swear so much,' he answered.

Now compare your reactions to the passage with the following, gleaned from a number of different adults on various occasions. The notes are, like a cast list, in order of appearance:

1   Some people found the expression 'my spending Sunday' unusual. One young person thought it was a grammatical error. This formal, rather literary usage is not very fashionable at the moment, so it presented some readers with a syntactic difficulty, i.e. a problem with understanding how the words were connected together in a sentence to make a meaning.

2   'We did Little Hull': although the individual words made sense, many people were confused because it is slang to say you 'did' a town and Hull is a big place This is an example of two different problems, one of usage and one of context.

3   'Sink', 'pitch' and 'rack' all presented readers with vocabulary difficulties, because these were familiar words being used in a new way. The meanings they had did not work in this story.

4   'Petzl stop' was not understood by many people because it was vocabulary connected to the subject area. If they did not already know about this subject, readers had no way of understanding the words. The passage contains other examples of subject-specific vocabulary, including 'belays' and 'one-wall traverse'.

5   'It was only a one-wall traverse': readers were too confused to decide whether to take this at face value or read it as irony. This is an example of how difficulties in reading mount up, so that even quite small problems are intensified, making the meaning impenetrable.

6   'Crabs' was doubly confusing. It is a slang word used only by certain groups of people. More readers may have been familiar with the original word, karabiner.

7   'Cows' tails' presented particular problems because it sounds like a slang or joke phrase but there is no other expression used to describe this home-made piece of equipment.

8   'The patience of a cross-stitcher' may be a new phrase, but not everybody can cope with cross-stitching, you know. There's nothing wrong with that phrase, it just looks strange because it has been used instead of the more common 'patience of a saint'. If you did not know English idioms very well, you might well have wondered what saints had to do with it all. This is an example of a very common problem. Long-term English speakers may be so accustomed to some well-established expressions that they will not even notice them.

The passage was designed to give adult fluent users of English an opportunity to experience a few of the comprehension problems affecting later-stage bilingual learners. Readers experience the problems with vocabulary and feel disoriented by the oddities of syntax and idiom. If you have experienced some of these, imagine being in a classroom where your peers seem to have few problems with the passage. They may have to check out the more obscure items of technical vocabulary, but then, your teacher had guessed that in advance and came prepared. Your other problems do not seem such an issue to them. Now look at the following items, which could add to the syntactic difficulties of the passage for the less fluent:

1   The use of the passive voice in 'something was being rigged'. Does this mean something is doing rigging or that somebody is rigging something?

2   Some tenses, as in 'they had dragged me down'. Does this mean that a dragged-me-down is something they had, perhaps stored in a little bag?

3   Metaphors: did they really drag that poor woman? By her hair?

4   Conditionals, as in 'You would not have come if we had told you'. Take a moment to unpick this. There are four variables at work in one short sentence: a person coming or not coming, and people telling or not telling. All that differentiates any one outcome from another is a slight change: 'You would have come if we had not told you' has just got one word moved a little to the right-hand side. Even more interesting (if you like words) is looking at that sentence from a vocabulary point of view. There aren't any nice, meaty nouns or adjectives in there. The only verbs are 'come' and 'tell'. On one level, that sentence looks like: come + if + tell. The rest is just a bit of grammar. For people with a shaky hold on English grammar, that will make it a very difficult sentence indeed.

5   Shortening, e.g. 'When, in a state of shock and exhaustion, I collapsed . . .' This is a fancy way of pointing out that the writer collapsed and was in a bit of a state and then something else happened. Expressed in the fancy way, it makes for a more interesting read, but the text becomes 'dense'. Compare the full version: 'I collapsed. I was terrified and exhausted. I was on safe ground. Stephen said . . .' The fancy version omits all the repetitive stuff; it is packed with more meaning in less space. That makes it hard to read.

Now we have examined why nobody could understand a word of this perfectly correct, perfectly logical English passage, we will compare it to an easier piece. It will help if, as you read, you spot which parts of the text support your understanding.

Sundays in the dark

I used to go caving, but I was never very good at it. A lot of the time, I was the only woman and I was older and smaller than the others. Some of my friends used to envy my spending Sunday with a bunch of beefy young men, but it had its drawbacks.

An example of this was the time we did Little Hull Pot.

It was a walk-in entrance, I remember, which made a pleasant change from some of the dangerous sink holes they had dragged me down. There was a short pitch near the entrance. I abseiled down using a tool called a petzl stop. I don't like a figure of eight descender and a rack goes too fast. There was quite a delay while the leaders rigged some obstacle ahead. I was in the passage, so I couldn't see. The queue of cavers in front of me started moving on after a while. When my turn came, I stepped up to the rigging. It was a one-wall traverse. The rock floor was one hundred feet below me. I showed remarkable self-restraint.

'You never told me that was there,' I said, politely.

'You would not have come if we had told you,' Mick replied, logically. He was right. I knew my limitations.

My choice was a simple one: press on, or get hypothermia waiting for four hours. With a sinking stomach, I unravelled my safety ropes and clipped my karabiners to the rope.

The traverse was about six or eight feet across, so there were a few belays: places where the rope was hooked up. These were hard to cross.

I inched along, tiring my arm muscles by hanging on too tightly. One of my safety ropes was too short, which made it even harder.

Mick was a very patient, kind person. He talked me through every movement. I depended on him completely. I was both embarrassed and terrified. I was also jealous of the ease with which Stephen was completing the traverse, just behind me.

When, in a state of shock and exhaustion, I collapsed on the safe ground beyond, Stephen said, 'You know, you really impressed me.' This was a novel idea. 'Why on earth is that?' I asked.

'Because I have never heard a lady swear so much,' he answered.

The same groups of readers identified the following features which made this passage easier:

1   The layout was felt to be more sympathetic. There were clear breaks. Text was arranged in bite-sized chunks which were still logically arranged, fairly conventional paragraphs.

2   The title was more pictorial, less cryptic.

3   The first paragraph set the scene. It built a bridge between the reader and the text. This is sometimes called 'foregrounding'.

4   There were physical details, such as 'the rock floor was one hundred feet below me'. These helped readers to form a picture of the incident.

5   Some technical terms were explained, e.g. 'a tool called a petzl stop'.

6   Some of the most confusing vocabulary had been changed or omitted. 'Cows' tails' made the interesting change to 'safety rope'. As was mentioned before, there is no alternative expression used by cavers. 'Safety rope' was put in as a generic term, because it was more obvious. This would help all readers, except, of course, cavers, who would wonder why the person in the story was not using cows' tails!

A teacher presenting the passage would have made comprehension even easier with diagrams, pictures and word lists. No doubt an outstanding teacher would have popped down Little Hull Pot on the end of a rope and taken a few photos.

The passages above should help teachers to understand some reading difficulties faced by their pupils with EAL. They may help when teachers vet resources or make their own. Later, we will look at some ways of using existing resources, as we often have to use things we regard as not quite right, simply because there is no alternative. In those instances, it's not what you use, but the way that you use it, that gets results. First, a few words about the pupils.

The client group

Pupils at Step 6 have been described as 'invisible' because their needs are so easily overlooked. A frequently made comment is that these pupils are performing better than some of their monolingual peers, or that their monolingual classmates show similar problems with academic English, therefore the bilingual pupil is the same as everyone else. Many teachers, when reading the passages above, will have felt that some monolingual pupils also have similar difficulties to those faced by later-stage bilinguals.

Parts of this are often true. There is an interesting debate about the precise differences in need or in language development between developing bilinguals and some monolingual pupils. Tempting as it is, contributing to that debate will not help teachers to decide what to do in the classroom tomorrow morning. We will therefore address the issue only in terms of practicalities, and leave the debate for another forum.

First, there are many reasons why a monolingual pupil may exhibit a low Cognitive Academic Language Proficiency:

- Low ability.
- Low motivation – lack of interest in some areas.
- Lack of examples in the home – not much chat or discussion in the family, not much reading in the family.
- Extreme shyness or lack of confidence – pupil stays on safe, simple levels.

All the above could be true of a bilingual pupil, but such a pupil could also have some or all of these characteristics:

- The pupil is developing these skills over a reduced number of years, having been using English for fewer years than his/her monolingual peers.
- The only place where this pupil is exposed to English is the classroom, therefore that is the only place where these skills can be developed in English.
- The pupil is developing these skills at home, but in a different language.
- The pupil exhibits some of these skills but cannot use them fully because s/he is operating in a different knowledge system.
- The pupil has more difficulties with complex syntax than his/her monolingual peers.

It would also be naive to assume that every single bilingual pupil in the education system is desperately in need of some kind of syntactic salvation. Some bilingual families are extremely efficient language users across the board and may justly resent such an assumption.

As usual, the real life patterns in a real classroom are messy. It would take longer to pick apart the different reasons why x struggles with z than it would to teach the pupils. The following, two-pronged approach is far more efficient. It avoids the dreaded SEEMS OK trap while saving the teacher unnecessary worry.

1 First prong: Keep details of the bilingual pupils in your class. Know which other languages they speak and which Step they are working on. Take this into account when planning lessons.

2 Second prong: Plan *all* lessons (no matter what subject area) through a filter of language needs and language development. If you are planning for language needs and language development, you will meet the needs of all the pupils in your class, whether bilingual or monolingual.

The core message is still: 'What is good for bilingual learners is good for everyone else, but not always vice-versa.'

Planning for language

Planning for language is merely a case of answering these questions:

- What are the difficulties inherent to this unit?
- What opportunities does this unit present to develop language skills?

The following examples from Key Stage 3 History illustrate how this works in practice.

A version of 'hot seating'

The class is told they are going to become journalists. They will be interviewing Queen Elizabeth I. Questions of varying complexity are modelled by the teacher. The class discusses the differences between the straightforward and the open-ended types of question. Questions are dissected for the class to see what patterns are common. They are given time in groups to prepare a mixture of different kinds of questions, which they could ask in their roles as journalists. When we did this, Queen Elizabeth was played by a teacher wearing a bit of make-up. It was not at all convincing, but it did add a sense of occasion. The pupils took it in turns to ask questions, and all took notes of the information given in reply. Depending on the situation and the teacher's aims, this stage could be organised in different ways. Each group could have its own Queen Elizabeth, for example, if enough pupils could manage this role. Of course, for this version of hot seating, they would need to answer accurately. We decided that using a teacher gave better control of the information and the pace of work.

Once the pupils have answers to their questions, they begin the next stage. The teacher shows an example of a newspaper interview and uses it to identify the key features of expression and organisation. The pupils set about writing up their own interviews, using the information gathered in the hot seating session. Differentiation is easy as the results can range from a simple tabloid-style Q and A list to a Sunday supplement in-depth spread. Once the drafts are completed, the pupils are put in pairs to act as editors for each other. They read each other's work, spot errors and suggest improvements. We had had enough by this stage, but there is plenty of scope for good ICT work in this, especially if the pupils draft their pieces on the PC.

Hot seating has been well known for many years, but it takes on another dimension when the teacher plans for language. The nature of asking and composing questions is thoroughly explored, as are the features of newspaper interviews.

Sorting

The class was given a sequence of pictures. When put in the right order, they illustrated the story of the Gunpowder Plot. Each picture had a caption, which explained the details. The class, therefore, started at the simplest level, i.e. just pictures, and then moved on to text, which was as complex or as brief as the teacher chose. Pupils with reading difficulties had cards containing a few words, while better readers could have paragraphs.

Putting everything together in this way is a popular activity in many subject areas. It is especially good when pupils are encouraged to work in groups or pairs; it uses talk, text and pictures so there are many ways of supporting meaning and going over the facts in an enjoyable way.

Looking at the language needs and language opportunities presented by this activity, we can see that on one level it is mostly about narrative: saying what happened and when, and perhaps adding a few descriptive elements about the nature of the buildings involved or the gory bits at the end. On a higher level, however, which is what we are interested in at the moment, this story will be all about reasons, causes and effects. We want the pupils to be able to give reasons for the gunpowder plot's conception, design and failure. In EAL-teaching terms, this means we want them to pick out the facts and understand them, and then express causality.

Once our pupils had put together the story, they were asked to make a list of the people in the story. We did this by going through the captions and marking the text. The pupils entered the names in a table like the one in Figure 8.1 below. They then filled in the second column, using a combination of reading, remembering earlier lessons and educated guesswork.

Once again, this kind of activity works better in groups. Because there is a heavy load of information to find before the sequence can move on, teachers can choose, at this stage, to let their pupils play 'industrial spy'. This is an old favourite in which each group can, on a given signal, send one member to visit another group to 'spy' on their work and return with any missing facts or clever ideas. During a lesson like this one, 'industrial spy' speeds up the fact-gathering part of the lesson. In another situation, it might help some groups to find inspiration, or to compare their work-rate.

Name	What did they want?	What did they do?
King James	He wanted England to be a Protestant country	
Guy Fawkes	He wanted to kill the King	
The person who wrote the letter to Monteagle		Warned him not to go to parliament

Figure 8.1 An example of the 'sorting' table, partially completed

Expressing information in table form separates the fact-finding from the fact-expressing. Therefore the pupils can concentrate on one task at a time. Once completed, the table can be used to create text. Teachers can scaffold the production of sentences in several ways, for example:

- 'The person who wrote to Monteagle warned him not to go to parliament in order to protect him.'
  This is made by using column 1, then column 3, then 'in order to', then column 2.
- King James wanted England to be a Protestant country, so he was hard on the Catholics.
  This is made by using columns 1 and 2, then 'so', then column 3.

Again, none of the ideas in this sequence is new. Putting them together in this way, however, facilitates first the removal of barriers to learning caused by difficulties with language, and then the development of some of the expressions pupils need if they are to achieve higher levels.

Adapting materials

Sometimes, we use what we know are dense texts or unattractive books simply because we have no option. On these occasions, there are things we can do to minimise the problems this may cause.

Text marking

There are many varieties of text-marking activities. Broadly speaking, they all involve finding information in a text, marking the place, and then doing something with what has been marked. Such activities are rightly popular at all levels of fluency and in a variety of situations. We give them a special mention in this context, however, because text marking enables the pupils to find the most important pieces of information without necessarily having to engage with the whole of an impenetrable lump of prose. If the pupils then use the marked places to create something, such as a table, diagram or summary, they will have effectively replaced the text with a more useful record of their own. The fullest expression of this kind of strategy is probably found in *Extending Literacy* by David Wray and Maureen Lewis (Wray and Lewis 1997a).

Modelled reading

If you have not tried this before, it takes a little practice. It is, however, a powerful strategy which has the added bonus of being cheap in terms of both time and resources. Put simply, the teacher reads the passage to the class while showing them how he has interacted with the text to understand it. This may involve checking back to identify what a pronoun means. For example, in this passage, 'he' refers to 'the teacher'. It may also involve modelling the use of a dictionary to look up, perhaps 'pronoun'. It could also involve vocalising the sort of dialogue a good reader has with print, such as 'I'm not sure I agree with that', 'We need to remember that next time we put sodium in water', or 'I saw one of those last week in Dudley'. The most effective way of modelling reading is to have the text projected on to a screen, if possible. The benefits of this technique are that, as well as being able to use a text you might not otherwise have chosen, most importantly, you are teaching the pupils how to become effective readers as well as sharing with them the content of the text.

Text deconstruction

This sounds rather grand in a postmodernist way, but it is really a progression from modelled reading. Again, it is a well-used strategy in its own right, but we are mentioning it here because it is so useful where resources are scarce. For this, the teacher shows the class how the text is made up of parts, each with a separate task to do (such as introducing a topic or describing a procedure). Working with a text in this way, it becomes easy to spot certain words or phrases that do special jobs. Examples of these include 'however', 'in the event of', 'nevertheless', etc. These are linking devices which guide us through the logic of a text. Identifying the different parts of a text exposes these linking words or phrases in action, illustrating their meanings very effectively. Text deconstruction is kin to 'scaffolding writing' which is based on the fact that, once the pupils understand how sections of a text work together and are linked together, they can use the links to create a text of their own. For a full description of scaffolding writing, we again refer to the work of Maureen Lewis and David Wray, this time in *Writing Frames* and *Writing Across the Curriculum*, both published in 1997 by the Reading and Language Information Centre, University of Reading.

CALP at Key Stage 1

Cognitive academic language proficiency is not necessarily age dependent, but relies more on understanding of concepts. Activities can be set up which will allow young learners to develop their ability to express complex, multilayered concepts and ideas, based on their own prior knowledge and experiences. Such activities, which may be primarily oral, can provide the foundations for a more formal approach through writing. This same approach is equally supportive of older learners, whose conceptual development may be more sophisticated, but who need to practise manipulating ideas and linking layers of thinking before putting these into writing.

Example

Group of eight pupils (three with EAL) from Year 2 class. Subject: 'People from History'

A very stereotypical picture of Louis Pasteur wearing a white coat and handling glass scientific equipment was provided, along with an equally stereotypical picture of Edward Jenner seated by a desk, apparently talking to a woman and a child while examining the child's arm.

Two basic information sheets, one about Jenner and the other about Pasteur, were cut into sentence strips and mixed up. The task for the group was to read the text and match it to the right picture. The teacher observed and intervened on occasions to develop ideas being put forward.

This is the sort of exchange which took place:

Pupil 1:	'I think he's a scientist.' [pointing to picture of LP]
Pupil 2:	'Yeh, he's wearing a white coat.'
Teacher:	'Don't doctors wear white coats?'
Pupil 2:	'Not all the time, anyway, I think he's the doctor.' [pointing to picture of EJ]
Pupil 3:	'Yeh, me too.'
Teacher:	'Why do you think that?'
Pupil 3:	'Because there's a lady there with a little boy, she looks like she's talking to the doctor.'
Teacher:	'What makes you think he might be a doctor?'
Pupil 3:	'Because it's like when I go to the doctor – my mum takes me and the doctor is behind the desk.'

During these exchanges the young pupils were given opportunities to state their opinions, and to justify them using their own criteria.

Sorting the text gave rise to some interesting comments. For example, on sentence strips *'Louis Pasteur was a scientist'*, *'Edward Jenner was a doctor'*, the children placed the strips under the correct pictures, after the exchange outlined above. However, placing *'He lived a long time ago in England'* and *'He lived a long time ago in France'* was more problematic. They eventually decided in which countries the two men lived by drawing on their knowledge of English spelling conventions – *'His name's spelt different, so he's French'* (of Louis Pasteur).

They made semantic links tied in to their own prior knowledge – *'Edward lived in the country and looked after people who worked on farms'* led them to make the connection with milkmaids and cows, and their initial sort of the sentences was based on looking for these key words. They included 'milk' in these key words at first, which led to more discussion and searching for clues as they realised it did not fit with the writing on Edward Jenner.

The activity enabled these young pupils to both demonstrate and practise manipulating their higher-order thinking abilities, because:

- the visual element set an immediate context;
- the reasoning aspects of the activity were primarily oral;
- the pupils were able to spark ideas off one another and extend each other's thinking;
- two very stereotypical pictures ensured the field of discussion was contained;
- the structure of the text ensured that there were sufficient clues to complete the task successfully, but with some ambiguities to generate discussion;
- the teacher extended the discussion with open-ended questions.

Developing independence

Supportive arrangements for later stage learners are likely to be useful for monolingual pupils as well. They include:

1   Use of learning mentors to talk over problems, to advise on organisation and to explain systems. Learning mentors can be a bridge between an individual pupil and the workings of a busy institution, explaining the motivations of each to the other. They can also approach the curriculum from the pupil's point of view, using previous knowledge to make sense of new content. Mentors can also draw together threads from separate areas or coach in common skills needed in different subjects; a facility of special benefit at Key Stage 3 or 4.

2   Showing and deconstructing finished products/assignments. As well as giving pupils an idea of what standard they are aiming for, showing a finished product is the most practical way of explaining what the task entails.

3   The use of graphic organisers and similar ways of reducing the pupil's cognitive load. Working with an organiser separates manipulation of concepts from the production of complex language forms. The pupil may be able to perform both these tasks, but not always at the same time.

Accompanying CD

The CD accompanying this book contains a number of downloadable and amendable resources for readers in the purchasing organisation to use.

Booklets and handouts

1. Activities with a picture
2. Blackpool's 'Race Equality in the Classroom' document
3. Encouraging English Language Development
4. Handout on using interpreters
5. Parachute games
6. Preparing a topic
7. Reading with bilingual learners
8. Using a card reader
9. Using dual-text resources

Materials for training

10, 11. Blackpool's speech bubbles poster (see over)
12. Figure 2.2: A Model of Progress
13. Sundays in the Dark
14. Tales from a Misspent Middle Age
15. Teaching in Partnership Contract
16. The Partnership Cycle by NFER
17. ZPD Presentation

New admissions

18. Interpreting proforma
19. Questions for new admissions
20. Mid-term admission of bilingual pupils: flow chart

Teaching materials

21. Two-minute biography
21a. Fact sheets 1 (Jenner) 2 (Pasteur)
22. Music project group work
23. Science worksheets (digestion)
24. Activities based on the 'Owl babies'
25. Flashcards/labels

Examples of activities for the Panic File

26. Numbers 1
27. Numbers 2
28. Shapes 1, 2, 3
29. School equipment 1 & 2

30. Subjects
31. Subjects 2
32. Subjects 3
33. Subjects 4

34. Blank filling exercise (computer)
35. Label the computer

Blackpool's speech bubble poster (see CD)

Glossary

Note: These are our definitions of the following expressions as used in this book.

Advanced bilingual learners: These pupils have already acquired conversational English and are now acquiring the higher-order language skills so essential to access the curriculum. Typically these bilingual learners are operating beyond NASSEA Step 4.

BICS: Basic Interpersonal Communication Skills. A term coined by Jim Cummins. This is often tied in with social fluency because it has many features in common with the spoken, conversational or informal varieties of the language. BICS describes language which can be partially understood because of situational clues, gestures or facial expressions. This kind of language is typified by simple sentence structures with a lexicon similar to that of spoken language. It is used extensively as social language, but its academic use is confined to simpler purposes such as labelling, classifying and recounting.

Bilingual: This terminology is used when a pupil has to use more than one language. However, it does not mean to say the pupil is equally competent in both languages. Bilingual describes the situation the pupil is in. It does not refer to a level of fluency.

Buddy: A pupil who will support a fellow pupil during the settling-in process.

CALP: Cognitive Academic Language Proficiency. A term coined by Jim Cummins. This refers to a range of language concepts and skills which pupils need to formulate and discuss the abstract, the theoretical and the complex. CALP is also needed to express delicate nuances of thought. It is typified by the use of Latin-based vocabulary and sophisticated grammatical forms. CALP is used for academic purposes such as hypothesising, persuading, evaluating and deducing.

Context for learning: The situations which can affect the pupil's performance, e.g. a friendly class or a familiar topic.

Context for meaning: The information or situation which can affect meaning or make meaning clearer.

English as an Additional Language (EAL): Pupils whose preferred language/s are not English learn English and add it to their other language/s. This process is called learning EAL. At the same time, these pupils are learning the National Curriculum, which is taught in English. This is called learning through EAL.

Idiom: Like people, words and phrases have habits which do not necessarily follow a logical pattern. For example, 'It is raining cats and dogs' would make no sense if translated literally, but it is in such frequent use that it is not automatically recognised as a figurative expression.

Language function: A job that a piece of language does, e.g. to criticise, to narrate, to predict, to evaluate.

Moving target: As it takes a bilingual learner a number of years to acquire EAL and the monolingual pupils are making progress in English all the time, the bilingual pupils have to achieve more than their peers each year in order to catch up.

New to English: Describes a pupil (also called a beginner bilingual) who speaks no English as yet.

Peer tutoring: A more advanced pupil working with or helping another pupil.

Preferred language: The language a bilingual pupil feels the most comfortable with. This may be different for different tasks. It may not be the first language the pupil learned. Many bilingual pupils are actually multilingual because they use more than two languages.

Scaffolding support: This is the support given to a pupil to enable him/her to function at a higher level. It could be one of a number of strategies, including use of a writing frame or oral rehearsal for written work.

Silent period: This is the time when a pupil new to English does not speak, but listens attentively. Some pupils have an extended silent period. This is normal developmental behaviour and should not be regarded as a sign of learning difficulties.

Structure: An English structure is an example of a grammatical form. For example, conditionals are structures. We say 'I am taller than you'. The same pattern makes 'I am fatter than Fred' and 'I am smarter than the average bear'. The structure that makes these sentences is 'I am ___ er than N'. Structures can be isolated, discussed and practised to help pupils acquire EAL.

Subject-specific vocabulary: Words which are only used or have a special meaning when used in a particular curriculum area. For example, 'crankshaft' is only used when talking about engines. 'Manifold' can have two meanings: one is subject specific to machinery, the other just means 'many'.

Syntax: This refers to the way strings of words are connected together to make meaning. This is sometimes called 'grammar' but it should not be confused with notions of grammar concerned with getting full stops in the right places or with not splitting infinitives.

Utterances: Anything spoken. Some linguists use this term rather than 'sentences' as we clearly do not speak in sentences like those we write.

Bibliography

Asher, J. (1994) *Round the World Cookbook.* Cambridge: Longman.

Bernstein, B. (1974) *Class, Codes and Control.* London: Routledge and Kegan Paul.

Brent Language Service (2002) *Enriching Literacy – Text, Talk and Tales in Today's Classroom,* 2nd edn. Stoke on Trent: Trentham Books.

Cooke, S. (1997) *Collaborative Learning Activities in the Classroom: Designing inclusive materials for learning and language development.* Leicester: Resource Centre for Multicultural Education.

Cummins, J. (1996) *Negotiating Identities: Education for empowerment in a diverse society,* 2nd edn 2001. Los Angeles: California Association for Bilingual Learners.

Cummins, J. (2000) *Language, Power and Pedagogy, Bilingual Children in the Crossfire.* Clevedon: Multilingual Matters.

Edwards, V. (1998) *The Power of Babel: Teaching and learning in multilingual classrooms.* Stoke on Trent: Trentham Books.

Fellowes, A. (2001) *Bilingual Shakespeare: A Practical Approach for Teachers.* Stoke on Trent: Trentham Books.

First Steps (1997a) *Oral Language Resource Book.* Melbourne: Rigby Heinemann.

First Steps (1997b) *Oral Language Developmental Continuum.* Melbourne: Rigby Heinemann.

Gibbons, P. (1993) *Learning to Learn in a Second Language.* Portsmouth, NH: Heinemann.

Gibbons, P. (2002) *Scaffolding Language: Scaffolding Learning, Teaching second language learners in the mainstream classroom.* Portsmouth, NH: Heinemann.

Gravelle, M. (1996) *Planning for Bilingual Learners: An Inclusive Curriculum.* Stoke on Trent: Trentham Books.

Gravelle, M. (2001) *Supporting Bilingual Learners in Schools.* Stoke on Trent: Trentham Books.

Gregory, E. (1996) *Making Sense of a New World: Learning to read in a second language.* London: Paul Chapman.

Holderness, J. and Lalljee, B. (1988) *An Introduction to Oracy.* London: Cassell.

McWilliam, N. (1998) *What's in a Word? Vocabulary development in multilingual classrooms.* Stoke on Trent: Trentham Books.

Maslow, A. (1987) *Motivation and Personality,* 3rd edn. London: HarperCollins.

NALDIC (1999) *The Distinctiveness of English as an Additional Language: A cross-curriculum discipline.* Working Paper 5.

NASSEA (2001) *EAL Assessment: Guidance on the NASSEA EAL Assessment System.*

NFER/DES (1990) *Partnership Education Pack.* London: HMSO.

Nyakatawa, S. and Siraj-Blatchford, I. (1994) 'Bilingualism, Biculturalism and Learning in Early Years Classrooms', in A. Blackledge (ed.), *Teaching Bilingual Children.* Stoke on Trent: Trentham Books, ch. 8.

O'Toole, M. and Coote, H. (1994) *Responding to Traditional Tales, Key Stage One.* London: Evans Brothers.

Pinker, S. (1994) *The Language Instinct.* London: Penguin.

Pinker, S. (forthcoming) 'Language Acquisition', in L. R. Gleitman, M. Liberman and D. N. Osherson (eds.), *An Invitation to Cognitive Science, Volume 1: Language,* 2nd edn. Cambridge, Mass.: MIT Press.

Primary National Strategy (2003) *Speaking, Listening, Learning: Working with children in Key Stages 1 and 2.* London: QCA.

QCA (2000) *A Language in Common.* London: QCA.

Race Relations Amendment Act (2000). London: HMSO.

Trudgill, P. (1975) *Accent, Dialect and the School.* London: Edward Arnold.

Vygotsky, L. S. (1986) *Thought and Language.* Cambridge, Mass.: MIT Press.

Wray, D. and Lewis, M. (1997a) *Extending Literacy.* London: Routledge.

Wray, D. and Lewis, M. (1997b) *Writing Frames: Scaffolding children's writing in a range of genres.* Reading: Reading and Language Information Centre, University of Reading.

Wray, D. and Lewis, M. (1997c) *Writing Across the Curriculum: Frames to support learning.* Reading: Reading and Language Information Centre, University of Reading.

Appendix: Finding out more

Useful contacts

Northern Association of Support Services for Equality and Achievement (NASSEA)
c/o Ethnic Minority Achievement Service
TEDC
Lakes Road
Dukinfield SK16 4TR
Tel: 0161 331 3153
Fax: 0161 331 3133
Website: www.nassea.org.uk

Midlands Association of Support Services for Equality and Achievement (MASSEA)
Minority Group Support Services
Prior Deram Walk
Canley
Coventry CV4 8FT
Tel: 024 7671 7800
Fax: 024 7671 7900

Association of Local Authority Officers for Multicultural Education (ALAOME)
c/o Chris Vieler-Porter
Evaluation, Advisory and Curriculum Services
Education Centre
Queens Road
Walthamstow
London E17 8QS

National Association for Language Development in the Curriculum (NALDIC)
Membership Secretary
School Cottage
Hollyfield Road
Surbiton
Surrey KT5 9AL
Website: www.naldic.org.uk

Collaborative Learning Project
c/o Stuart Scott
17 Barford Street
Islington
London N1 0QB
Tel: 020 7226 8885
Email: collearn@rmplc.co.uk
Website: www.collaborativelearning.org

National Association for the Teaching of English (NATE)
50 Broadfield Road
Sheffield S8 0XJ
Tel. 0114 255 5419
Fax: 0114 255 5296
Email: natehq@btconnect.com
Website: www.nate.org.uk

The Refugee Council
3 Bondway
London SW8 1SJ
Tel. 020 7820 3042
Fax: 020 7582 9929

Books and other resources

Trentham Books Limited
Westview House
734 London Road
Oakhill
Stoke on Trent
Staffordshire ST4 5NP
Tel: 01782 745567/844699
Fax: 01782 745553
Email: tb@trentham-books.co.uk
Website: www.trentham-books.co.uk

Milet Publishing
6 North End Parade
London W14 0SJ
Tel: 020 7603 5477
Fax: 020 7610 5475
Email: info@milet.com
Website: www.milet.com

Multicultural Book Services
Unit 3
Carlisle Business Centre
60 Carlisle Road
Bradford BD8 8BD
Tel/fax: 01274 544158
Mobile: 07980 420982
Email: aamirdarr@multiculturalbookservice.fsnet.co.uk

RDS
8 Merton Road
London E17 9DE
Tel/fax: 020 8521 6969
Email: r.desalvo@tesco.net
Website: www.rdsbooks.com

Roy Yates Books
Smallfield Cottage
Cox Green
Rudgwick
Horsham
RH12 3DE
Tel: 01403 822299
Fax: 01403 823012

Mantra Lingua
5 Alexander Grove
London N12 8NU
Tel: 020 8445 5123
Fax: 020 8446 7745
Email: info@mantralingua.com
Website: www.mantralingua.com

Nicholas Roberts Publications Ltd
2 The Courtyard
Main Road
Barleythorpe
Oakham LE15 7FZ
Tel: 01572 722444
Fax: 01572 757734
Website: www.art-of-writing.co.uk

The Festival Shop Ltd
56 Poplar Road
Kings Heath
Birmingham B14 7AG
Tel: 0121 444 0444
Fax: 0121 441 5404
Email: info@festivalshop.co.uk

Development Education Project
c/o Manchester Metropolitan University
801 Wilmslow Road
Didsbury
Manchester M20 2QR
Tel: 0161 445 2495
Website: www.dep.org.uk

Tamarind Limited
PO Box 52
Northwood
Middlesex HA6 1UN
Tel: 020 8866 8806
Email: info@tamarindbooks.co.uk
Website: www.tamarindbooks.co.uk

Lingua Language Services
4 Glenthorpe
Lamma Wells Road
Holmfirth
Huddersfield HD9 2SP
Tel: 01484 689494
Fax: 01484 689594
Email: lingua-uk@msn.com

Further reading

Alladina, Safder (1995) *Being Bilingual*. Stoke on Trent: Trentham Books.

Brent Language Service (2002) *Enriching Literacy – Text, Talk and Tales in Today's Classroom*. Stoke on Trent: Trentham Books.

Dadzie, Stella (2000) *Toolkit for Tackling Racism in Schools*. Stoke on Trent: Trentham Books.

Gibbons, Pauline (1991) *Learning to Learn in a Second Language*. Portsmouth, NH: Heinemann.

Gravelle, Maggie (2001) *Planning for Bilingual Learners*. Stoke on Trent: Trentham Books.

Websites

www.emaonline.org.uk – An on-line resource base and focal point.
www.literacytrust.org.uk

Index

academic English 43
  CALP 21, 22, 83–4, 88, 92–3
  social English and 19–20, 21, 22, 41, 42, 71, 72, 74
accuracy 14
active learning 74
adaptation 9–10, 11, 15, 91–2
admissions, mid-term
  admissions form 49, 50, 52
  buddy systems 54–6
  groundwork 51, 53
  ideal set-up 58, 59
  interpreters 49, 56–8, 59
  panic file 53–4
  parent meetings 49, 51
  review 60
  time factors 58
admissions form 50, 52
advanced learners 39–42
age 12, 13
alienation 21, 46, 48
anti-racism 6–7, 8
anxiety 45, 53–4
art 10, 12
assertiveness 1, 10, 12
assessment
  observation as 14, 21, 22, 23
  scope 21, 22
  by steps see NASSEA Steps
authenticity 4–5

Basic Interpersonal Communication Skills (BICS) 21, 22
beginners 1, 2–5, 6–7, 10, 12, 14–15, 27–30, 60–6, 69–70
  hierarchy of needs 45–9, 57–8
  mid-term admissions 49–60
  misconceptions on 45
belonging 48
bias 69, 82
BICS (Basic Interpersonal Communication Skills) 21, 22
books 30, 36
buddy systems 54–6

CALP (Cognitive Academic Language Proficiency) 21, 22, 83–4, 88, 92–3
cognitive framework 2–5

collaboration 75–6
  group work 6, 27, 32, 35, 51, 53, 62, 63–6, 79–82, 90
  partnership 5–6
  shared activities 33, 63–4, 65, 80
comfort, physical 46
communication 11, 74 see also individual terms
communities 20–1
comprehension 7, 10, 12, 33, 36, 84–8
computer programs 54
conceptual skills 92–3
concrete learning 78
condensed text 86
confidence 34, 56, 72
  misconceptions on 71
context 15–18, 84, 85, 86, 87
conversation see social English
cross-curricular skills ix, 14, 22, 78–9
cultural factors 46
  misconceptions on 1, 20–1
  multiculturalism 2, 4–5, 48
Cummins, Jim 2–4
curriculum 25, 26 see also individual terms

deconstructing text 92
differentiation 29, 32, 64–6, 71–2
disruption 14–15, 46, 48

EAL (English as an Additional Language) vii, ix, 7–8, 96 see also individual terms
empowerment 2
engagement 4–5, 74
English ix, 66 see also individual terms
English as an Additional Language (EAL) vii, ix, 7–8, 96 see also individual terms
envoy group work 81
established learners 34–6

flash cards 61, 62
fluency 39

GCSE 70
geography 9–10
group work 6, 27, 32, 35, 51, 53, 62, 63–6, 79–82, 90

handwriting 36
hierarchy of needs 45–9, 57–8
history 63–6, 89–91, 92–3

holistic practices vii, ix, 2–5, 15
hot seating 89–90

idioms 84, 85–6, 87
independence 9, 12–13, 44, 93–4
individual learners vii, 2
industrial spy group work 90
insensitivity 1
intelligibility 29, 69, 84–8
intermediate learners 37–9, 71–3, 74–9
interpreters 49
    hierarchy of needs and 57–8
    recording by 59
    scope 56–7, 58
    time factors 57, 58

jigsaw group work 64–6, 81
jigsaw puzzlers 4, 61

Key Stages
    beginners 61–6, 69–70
    CALP 92–3
knowledge vii–ix, 27, 34, 51

language behaviour 10–15 see also individual
    terms
'Language in Common, A' (QCA) 22–3
listening 34–5, 79, 80
    primacy 24, 74
listening triads 80
lists 63–4

marking text 91
Maslow, Abraham 45–6, 47
materials see resources
medical information 52
mentors 94
mime 62
mirroring 33
mobility 46
modelling 27
    of reading 91–2
moving target 73, 83, 88
multiculturalism 2, 4–5, 48

naming 61, 62
NASSEA (Northern Association of Support
    Services for Equality and Achievement)
    Steps 22, 23, 24
    Step 1 27–30, 60–1
    Step 2 30–3
    Step 3 34–6
    Step 4 37–9, 71–3, 74–9
    Step 5 39–42
    Step 6 42–4, 88–9
    Step 7 44
Negotiating Identities (Cummins) 2
Northern Association of Support Services for
    Equality and Achievement see NASSEA
    Steps
number work 54

observation 14, 21, 22, 23

oracy see speech
overload 73, 74–5, 83, 88

panic file 53–4
paper-based activities 39
parents 49, 51
parity 42–4, 88–9
partnership 5–6
partnership cycle 5–6
peer tutoring 78
phonics skills 36
photographs 62
phrase development 30–3
pictures 90, 92–3
planning 89–91
points of view group work 81–2
posters 63, 65
praise 33
preferred languages 25, 29, 52, 56, 73–4,
    88
    books with 30
    misconceptions on 49, 51
Primary National Strategy 78–9
progress 12–13, 14, 15, 21, 22, 55–6
    misconceptions on 71–2, 73, 83–4, 88

QCA (Qualifications and Curriculum Authority)
    Steps 22–3, 24
    NASSEA Steps from see NASSEA Steps
questioning 29, 89–90

Race Relations (Amendment) Act 2000 6–7
rainbow group work 81
reading 36, 40, 43, 84–8, 91–2
    primacy 24, 30
    shared 33
recording 59
religious information 52
resources 30, 33, 36, 39, 53, 81, 82, 87–8
    adaptation 91–2
    bias 69
    computer programs 54
    intelligibility 69
    scope 69
    Speaking, Listening, Learning 78–9
    visual aids 25, 29, 30, 54, 61–2, 63, 65, 66, 69,
        90, 92–3
respite activities 30, 53–4
review 60
routine 7

safety 7, 46
scaffolding vii–viii, 38, 72, 91
    of writing 92
science 72, 76–8, 92–3
security 7, 46
self-esteem 48, 56
semantics 33, 36, 84–8
sentences 33, 77
sequencing 36, 61–3, 75–6, 90–1
sequencing cards 36
shared information 63–4, 65, 80
shared reading 33

silent periods 10, 12, 14, 29
  misconceptions on 20
slang 84, 85, 86
snowball group work 63–4, 80
social English 27
  academic English and 19–20, 21, 22, 41, 42, 71, 72, 74
  BICS 21, 22
  limitations 19–21
socio-economic factors 20–1, 46
sorting 61, 90–1
speech 36, 79, 82, 96
  primacy 24, 72–4
  scope 75–7
  social English see social English
Speaking, Listening, Learning (Primary National
    Strategy) 78–9
stress 45, 53–4
support 42
  buddy systems 54–6
  collaboration see collaboration
  mentors 94
  misconceptions on 67, 68
  peer tutoring 78
  primacy 68–9
  scaffolding vii–viii, 38, 72, 91, 92
  scope 49, 67–8, 93–4

syntax 37, 84, 85–6

table work 90–1
tableaux group work 66
tailoring 89
target setting 24–5 see also individual terms
TAs (teaching assistants) 67–9
transformation of information 27
truth 69, 82

verb tenses 86
visual aids 25, 29, 30, 54, 61–2, 63, 65, 66, 69, 90, 92–3
visual clues 10, 12, 14, 16
vocabulary 36, 61, 62, 76, 77, 84–5, 86, 87

wall displays 66
whole-school practices vii
worksheets 54, 66
writing 38, 40, 43, 92
  academic English see academic English
  misconceptions on 71–2
  primacy 24
  scope 77–8

ZPD (Zone of Proximal Development) vii–viii, 73